Prelude

THE GREATEST MUSIC ever written. The greatest composers the world has ever known. Their oratorios have brought audiences to tears. Their symphonies have brought royalty to their feet shouting bravo and demanding encores. Cities have built great concert halls simply to enhance their genius. And now, one man brings you their story in a book you are destined to treasure. As much a classic as the musicians who have set the stage for mankind, the *Wannabe Guide to Classical Music* is a testimony to the literary gifts of an author certain to find his own place in history. RDR Books is proud to introduce Robert S. Wieder.

Wannabe Guide to

CLASSICAL
MUSIC

ROBERT S. WIEDER

RDR Books
Berkeley, California

Wannabe Guide to Classical Music

RDR Books
4456 Piedmont
Oakland, California 94611

First Edition

ISBN 1-57143-055-5

Library of Congress Catalog Card Number 2001096155

Cover Design: Jennifer Braham
Book Design: Paula Morrison
Editor: Bob Drews
Assistant Editor: Kim Klescewski
Illustrations: Sergei Ponomarov
Researchers: Julie Wulfheider, Kristin Burke, Jonathan Rapoport

The Berkeley Public Library generously assisted the author on this
project.

Distributed in England and Europe by Airlift Book Company,
8 The Arena, Mollison Avenue, Enfield, Middlesex EN3 7NJ England

Printed in Canada.

Contents

Introduction: What Is Classical Music and Why Do You Want to Learn More about It?

WHAT IS CLASSICAL MUSIC? This is not as cut-and-dried as you might think. For one thing, if you take a half-dozen or so people at random and ask them, "What is classical music?" you are likely to get a half-dozen or so different answers, and that doesn't even include "Get lost."

1. "It's music composed roughly between 1750 and 1820."
2. "It's music where a guy has to conduct an orchestra."
3. "It's anything that includes violins."
4. "It's stuff by dead white Europeans."
5. "It's music from the period starting 1650 to around 1900."
6. "It's music that old people listen to."
7. "It's anything you play wearing a suit."
8. "It's, like, Sinatra and them, right?"

To many people, classical music is basically any music that was written and performed before they were born. The reality is, there's a lot of truth to several of these answers—especially numbers 2, 3, and 4—and at least some truth to almost all of them. But the most precise answer according to those who really know the subject is number 1.

Most people, however, *don't* really know the subject, and based on what *they* would call "classical" upon hearing it, the better answer might be number 5.

If this seems confusing, blame musical historians, who have divided classical music in general into seven historical periods, each with its own characteristic style of composing: Medieval (up to 1400), Renaissance (1400–1650), Baroque (1650–1750), Classical (1750–1820), Romantic (1820–1900), Impressionist (1870–1915), and Modern (1910–present).

As you can see, they've given us a situation where there are all kinds of classical music, but only one of which is called "Classical music." You don't usually see this kind of pointless confusion outside of government or your workplace.

Our book's solution to this problem is to define "classical" as *the kind of music created by those great and famous composers of the past whom the average person recognizes by name and thinks, "Oh yeah, classical music."* That would be Bach, Beethoven, Mozart, Brahms, Wagner, Tchaikovsky, and their various peers and colleagues.

By that measure, classical music will include the Baroque period (Bach), the Classical period (Mozart, Beethoven), and the Romantic period (Brahms, Wagner, Tchaikovsky). Admittedly, that will give short shrift to some stellar composers: Impressionists like Debussy and Ravel, and Moderns like Bartok and Shostakovich. Alas, life—and this book—aren't perfect.

There are many persuasive arguments for learning about classical music, not the least of which is that it is a dazzling art form. But why you and why now? Perhaps you feel that you *need* to learn more about classical music to grow as a person, experience life more fully, or finally get over that country music that reminds you of whoever broke your heart.

Or perhaps it's because you've realized that, at a certain point in life, it becomes time to lose the beer-can hat, toss those Mötley Crüe CDs, and move on to a more sophisticated level of artistic involvement.

Or perhaps it's because a gorgeous woman you were talking to in a cocktail lounge walked away when the subject of Beethoven came up and you said that you liked it well enough but preferred Beethoven's Second because there were more Saint Bernards.

Maybe, just for a change, you would like to be the kind of person who hears the *William Tell Overture* and turns the conversation to Rossini (its composer, first name Gioacchino, a master of 19th-century Italian opera) instead of Tonto (the Lone Ranger's Native American sidekick).

But why doesn't really matter. The point is, you're going to give it a try. The good news is, you'll probably like it, and it might even be good for you. The even better news is, getting a handle (or even a Handel) on classical music is not investment banking. It's a manageable topic. It's also relatively inexpensive. If it turns out you don't have an ear for this, just return the CDs to the library. If you bought some, rewrap them and give them to your brother-in-law as a birthday gift.

Of course, we don't cover the subject exhaustively, because exhaustion is not our purpose. The goal is just enough understanding and familiarity to have some fun with it. Because classical music can be fun. A little listening, a little reading, and with any luck at all, you'll soon be ready and able to invite that special someone over, put a stack of *exactly the right* Mozart and Schubert and Tchaikovsky CDs on the player, light those votive candles, break out the good sherry, and party like it's 1799.

The fact is, you don't really even need this book if your objective is just to see if you like the music. You can do that quite simply by listening to some. It's available at music stores, in cassettes and CDs at most libraries, and on radio stations in most well-populated areas.

But "classical music" is more than just how it sounds. In a sense (admittedly a narrow sense), it's like baseball: Anyone can enjoy it just for the way it's played, but to really appreciate it and get the maximum pleasure out of it, the key is being knowledgeable about its rules, traditions, history, and hall-of-fame greats. Think of the sonata form as akin to the infield fly rule: not easy to understand, but worth the effort if you really want to know what's going on.

A History Lesson. Period.

WE'RE MOSTLY SKIPPING the Renaissance period, the time from 1400–1650 when court music started to rival religious music. But we should note that historically, classical music has some important roots there. It was during the Renaissance period that the system of writing music down was refined into the form we know it today.

Also, it was during the Renaissance that music began to make a transition from the pastime of cloistered monks, nuns, and wandering troubadours to the entertainment of royal courts. In short, music was elevated from a kind of talent or craft into a valued and respected art form. If you were good enough at it, you could make a nice buck off it, so right away, it had a future.

On a more technical level, the Renaissance introduced **polyphony**— not the opposite of polylegitimate, but the simultaneous blending of two or more melodies in harmony. The Baroque period would see composers expand, develop, refine, and very nearly beat the concept of polyphony to death.

The Baroque Period (1650–1750)

"Going for Baroque."
"If it ain't Baroque, don't fix it."
"Some composers followed the rules, others Baroque them."

Now that we've gotten all the bonehead puns out of the way, let's get down to business.

The big names were Johann Sebastian Bach, George Handel, and Antonio Vivaldi, although Johann Pachelbel would have perhaps the single biggest "hit" over the long run with his *Canon* (see "If It Sounds Familiar ..."). If Baroque music could be described in one word, the word would be "elaborate." Or maybe just "busy." The idea seemed to be "Why use just one note when you can pack in three or four?"

Baroque composers created some of classical music's most timeless melodies. Many of them, particularly the religious works, remain in regular use today in hymns and chorales. Baroque music was generally frilly, ornate, hyperactive, and given to showy displays of virtuosity on the violin or keyboard. Even so, some of it was as aimless and drifting as current New Age music.

It was during the Baroque period that composers developed the opera, the concerto, and the oratorio. The **opera** is what Luciano Pavarotti does, and it's basically a play wherein the performers sing their lines to the accompaniment of an orchestra.

The **concerto** is a piece that features a solo instrument with the backing or accompaniment of the orchestra. In that sense, it is a sort of *solo concert*. It usually consists of three *movements,* which is also the basic structure of the sonata and the symphony. The central idea of the concerto is *contrast* — using two or more instruments or musical voices to play off of and thereby highlight one another. There is also the **concerto grosso,** which does not mean a concerto that disgusts the listener, but a concerto where a small *group* of instruments is featured in contrast with the larger orchestra. Bach's *Brandenburg Concertos* are the classic example of this classical form and should be on your "must hear" list.

The **oratorio** is a kind of concert hymn: A grand-scale religious work written for and performed by an orchestra, chorus, and solo vocalists. It could actually be any dramatic poem, but in practice outside England it was usually a religious story. Unlike opera, there are no costumes or scenery or swordfights or suicides; they just stand there and sing. Like opera, they usually make no sense whatsoever if you're only fluent in English. The oratorio example-of-choice is another Bach composition: *The Passion According to St. Matthew.*

Listener's Tip: If the keyboard sound that you hear isn't a piano but the more delicate-sounding harpsichord, the music is from the Baroque period. See why just below.

The Classical Period (1750–1820)

Here we find the real towering figures of classical music: Ludwig van Beethoven, Wolfgang Amadeus Mozart, and Franz Joseph Haydn—although, as was the case with the Baroque period, the single most widely known work may be Beethoven's *Fifth Symphony.* This was the period when classical music grew up and got serious; when all of the major forms of classical music—the opera, concerto, symphony, and string quartet—became unified by adopting the fundamental structure that classical music follows to this day: the **sonata form.** This is going to seem a bit complicated, but really, sonata big deal.

The sonata form is just a fixed format for structuring a musical composition. It consists of three parts, which the composer takes in order and which add up to a **movement.** (Each movement, in turn, is usually just one of several that, together, make up a larger composition, such as a symphony.)

The first part of the sonata is called the **exposition** or **statement.** Here the composer introduces the basic themes of the movement, using different instruments and/or keys to define, distinguish, and establish each one. The key of the piece is called the tonic—the key to which the piece must always return. In the second part, the **development,** the composer manipulates and tinkers with the themes, exploring the many possibilities and variations by shifting to different beats, moving away from the tonic key, changing the instrumentation, combining or intensifying melodies, and so on. As often as not, the themes are pitted against one another in a kind of struggle for dominance. Some composers became so experimental with these rules that audiences occasionally stormed out in protest. Beethoven especially emptied a lot of concert hall seats.

The final part, the **recapitulation** or **restatement,** takes you back to the opening themes all in the tonic key, but usually with new harmonies. Sometimes there is also a dramatic **coda** (Italian for "tail") at the finale to tie up loose ends and to make it clear to the listeners that the movement is over and it's time to shift position in their seats.

A Clarifying Note: The sonata form is not the same thing as the **sonata.** A sonata is a composition for just a few instruments that *follows* the sonata form. Almost all sonatas that are played by a full orchestra are **symphonies.**

Like Baroque music, the Classical period had at its center the idea of contrast. The difference is that classical composers took what had been a musical one-on-one game and turned it into a team effort, contrasting not just the melody with the bass, but several melodies with each other in various combinations.

Another departure from Baroque was provided by the development of the piano, which replaced the harpsichord as the designated keyboard instrument in the orchestra. The harpsichord had its charms, but it was basically a low-tech musical instrument that had no pedals, no volume control, and no way to sustain notes. The piano replaced the harpsichord's more metallic sound with the richer, deeper, more barrel-chested resonating sound that we know and love, despite what Elton John has done with it.

Other instruments were also added to the orchestra during this period. As a result, Classical music in general has a grander feel and volume and tends to call forth descriptive phrases like "elegance and passion," "scope and grandeur," and "pomp and circumstance." (Well, "pomp," anyway.) If the defining musical form of the Baroque period was chamber music (and it was, we swear, on our coda honor, see page 50), the defining forms of the Classical period were the opera, the concerto, and the symphony.

The first great figure of the Classical period was Franz Joseph Haydn, who is known as the "Father of the Symphony." Given that he produced 104 of them it certainly beats being the Mother of the Symphony. His early symphonies and quartets (music written for four string instruments) were among the first to define the sonata form. A young Mozart admired him and went on to refine the symphony to near perfection, but as fate would have it, the teacher outlived his pupil by 18 years and Haydn's later works would show the influence of the man he taught.

The Hall of Fame compositions from the Classical period include Mozart's *Eine Kleine Nachtmusik* and *The Marriage of Figaro,* Rossini's *William Tell Overture,* Haydn's *London Symphony (No. 104),* and Beethoven's *Moonlight Sonata* and *Fifth Symphony.*

The Romantic Period (1820–1900)

If this period were a Great Composers' bus, you wouldn't be able to find an empty seat. Just *some* of the marquee-name Romantic composers were: Franz Schubert, Frederic Chopin, Robert Schumann, Felix Mendelssohn, Franz Liszt, Johannes Brahms, Giuseppe Verdi, Richard Wagner, Peter Tchaikovsky, Gustav Mahler, Jacques Offenbach, and at least two unrelated Strausses, Johann and Richard. Most experts would also include Beethoven, on the basis of his later-life work, as a composer who straddled both periods.

You could say that the Romantic period is when classical music became more democratic thanks in part to Mozart and Beethoven. In the first two decades of the 19th century, music spread from the courts and salons into the middle-class marketplace. A composer's popularity became a factor, and music experienced its very first craze: the waltz.

What primarily distinguishes the music of the Romantic period is a shift from artistic regimentation to individualism. Classical classical was characterized by the composers' subservience to order and symmetry and structure. Romantic classical, by comparison, was marked by composers turning away from the goal of technical perfection and instead emphasizing uniqueness, personal self-expression, and raw emotion. The idea wasn't so much to master the sonata form as to customize or embellish it, to give it life.

For most composers, this just meant getting frisky with

the rules, but a few radicals sometimes abandoned the old order completely, to write "free form" compositions that attempted to tell a story in sound. The key innovator in this regard was Liszt, who invented the **symphonic** (or **tone**) **poem**, in which the music was designed to convey a sense of the actual events in the story it was based on. For example, his *Dante Symphony* attempted to translate Dante's epic poem *The Divine Comedy* into music verse by verse, using instruments to express the cries of the damned, the lamentations of the wretched loveless, and other cheery elements of everlasting hell.

The label of Romantic for this period is no accident: The music of the time was often sighing, weepy, longing, idyllic, and languid. Really languid. Some of Liszt's more moody piano pieces could bore a clam. But Romantic classical music was also about passion and intensity, especially in the symphonies, where the idea seemed to be, "Why whisper a phrase when you can use the public address system?" Romantic composers waved their visions, their torments, and their ideals around like they were those big styrofoam *We're #1* hands at football games.

Orchestras expanded from 20 or so instruments to 100 and more. The more instruments you had to work with, the more emotions you could express. And the more that you could wring out of each instrument, the better, which meant that individual virtuoso violinists, pianists, and others were pushed to the limits of their ability by incredibly challenging solo parts. This, of course, was way before they had unions.

Symphonies grew longer, louder, more urgent, and flamboyant. It was music written and designed to fill a concert hall with sound and an audience with emotion. It was lush and soaring, or tortured and despairing, or neurotic and heroic.

It was exhausting. By 1870 it was wearing out its audiences and its welcome. Composers experimented with new ideas, sounds and inspirations, some from as far off as Indonesia and Africa. Those from less musically renowned countries, such as Grieg (Norway), Sibelius (Finland), and Dvorak (Bohemia), took nationalistic approaches. Ultimately, however, Romanticism was replaced by a return to simplicity and then a branching out into dozens of competing notions of "classical" music that still haven't sorted themselves out.

But for better or worse, the Romantic composers left us with the most memorable and recognizable melodies and individual works—the most classical "classics," if you will. A best-of-the-best list for this period would include Beethoven's *Ninth Symphony,* Liszt's *Hungarian Rhapsodies,* Chopin's *Polonaise No. 6,* Tchaikovsky's *1812 Overture* and *Romeo and Juliet,* Strauss's *Tales from the Vienna Woods,* and Wagner's *Die Walküre* and *Lohengrin.*

The Impressionist Period (1870–1915)

We said we wouldn't dwell on this, and we won't, but you never know when the subject might come up. So:

Classical music's relatively short-lived Impressionist period was a reaction against the gaudy, sentimental, breast-baring emotionalism of the Romantic period. Impressionism was virtually owned by a handful of composers—Claude Debussy, Maurice Ravel, and Frederick Delius. It abandoned complexity for simplicity, even minimalism. The idea was simply to *suggest* a landscape or herd of gazelles or picnic or boating accident or whatever your theme was, not to make a musical federal case out of it. There was no development stage, just a simple melodic idea offered up in a straightforward manner. Music was to be sensed, and heard, not thought about and analyzed. Form wasn't important, *sensibility* was. With Impressionist music, your imagination really pays off. There are no rules. You're on your own. Good luck. For a taste, the signature piece of Impressionism is Debussy's *Afternoon of a Faun.* The composer uses classical forms (like a set of variations) but draws you in with dream-like sequences.

The Modern Period (1910–Present)

Let's face it, "Modern classical" is an oxymoron. Basically, it means anything written since 1910 or so that uses an orchestra, instrumental group, or vocal group and calls itself "classical." It includes almost every musical form ever produced, from the jazz and ragtime influences in George Gershwin's sensational *Rhapsody in Blue* to the orchestral show tunes of Leonard Bernstein to the glorified Hungarian folk songs of Bela Bartok to the philharmonic square dances of Aaron Copland. There's a lot of marvelous stuff there, granted, but trying to categorize and make sense of it all is futile. There is no more "typical" Modern classical music than there is a typical mutation. Listen around; you'll know what you like.

Speaking of which, you like movies? Well, in a sense, you hear Modern classical music all the time if you're a freak for wide-scale, grandiose cinematic epics. If you sat and listened with your eyes closed to the sound track albums of such macro productions as *Ben-Hur, The Ten Commandments, The Right Stuff,* or *Lawrence of Arabia,* you'd be hard-pressed to distinguish them from some 19th-century composers of the Wagner school. You could also listen to Bernard Hermann who did many Hitchcock films, or Carl Stalling who did Warner Brothers' cartoons. The epic film score is, in a sense, the classical music of the 20th century, and there's probably no better example of this than the sound track written by the current master of the genre, a man named John Williams, for—don't laugh—the *Star Wars* series.

This hypothesis also goes both ways. Listen to certain 19th-century composers, and you can easily imagine their music backing up a chariot race or space battle or shark attack. There are Rimsky-Korsakov numbers that you would swear are straight from an Indiana Jones flick.

Hey, You've Gotta Hear This

THERE ARE CERTAIN PIECES of classical music that you really should listen to, in some cases because they are milestones in the history of musical creativity, in others because they just really sound cool. Think of them as classical music's Greatest All-Time Hits, and don't be surprised if they sound familiar the first time you play them.

Beethoven's *Fifth Symphony*—Probably the most famous and most widely popular major classical work, and maybe the one most often played and listened to, but definitely the one most easily and quickly identified, by its opening "dit-dit-dit-DAH."

Beethoven's *Ninth Symphony/Ode to Joy*—One of the all-time great examples of stretching a theme to its absolute limits in numerous directions, and almost impossible to sit still during when it heats up. Don't let your cardiac surgeon listen to it while he's giving you that bypass.

The only really memorable thing that Georges Bizet (1838–1875) composed was the opera *Carmen,* but as the saying goes, if you can only hit them once, make it a knockout punch. A true pop classical milestone, it all but transports you to Spain and shoves you in front of a bull. An outstanding example of various instruments each having their say with a distinct theme and fleshing it out.

Brahms' *Lullaby*—It is simply the definitive "baby's bedtime" theme music, which you may know with the words, "Hush a bye, and good night. . . . "

Dvorák's *Humoresque*—In the vaudeville era, this bouncy little staple item was the musical accompaniment to untold jugglers and acrobats. You're almost guaranteed to go, "Oh, that," the instant you hear it.

Handel's *Messiah*—Sort of the poinsettia of the classical music world: it is lovely and enjoyable in its own right, but whether you like it or not, it will be unavoidable during the Christmas holiday season. The Hallelujah Chorus is one of the supreme show-stoppers of the Baroque period (although it was never sung by the Supremes).

Liszt's Symphonic Poem Number 3, *Les Preludes,* is a gaudy, exultant horse race of a piece that sounds like he was watching a chase scene on TV while writing it, with some of the flat-out most rousing musical moments to come out of the 19th century.

Mendelssohn's *Hebrides Overture* is outstanding, and his *"Italian" Symphony No. 4* has a lively, prancing opening that may remind you of the theme to the "Dudley Do-Right" cartoons. If so, you're probably better off not mentioning it.

Should you be recalling a lost love or youth or happiness, or just in the process of getting on with your life on some level, Rachmaninoff's *Piano Concerto No. 2* is such a pure musical expression of *wistfulness* that you may want to make a point of listening to it—or, perhaps, of avoiding it.

Schubert's *Unfinished Symphony* has the advantage that, if you don't care for it, it only runs two movements long. Theories about *why* it is unfinished are easy to come by, the most likely being that it actually was finished, and the final two movements were simply lost by the man Schubert gave it to upon completion. The alternate theory—that he considered the first two movements so superb that he gave up trying to follow them—makes better conversation, but doesn't explain why he went on to write his *Ninth Symphony*, which, for good reasons, is known as Schubert's "Great" Symphony.

Schubert's *Symphony No. 2* is thoroughly rousing, and possibly even rip-roaring, but in any case so up tempo that the string section probably loses an aggregate 10 to 15 pounds performing it.

Scenes From Childhood by Robert Schumann is marvelous close-your-eyes-and-drift music. It captures a feeling of lazy, idyllic springtime and, in general, creates the distinct impression that little Bobby Schumann had it pretty good as a kid.

Strauss's *Blue Danube*—A terrific example of the purely evocative powers of great composing. You can almost see—and certainly feel—the flowing of a river, people leisurely bicycling, a carousel, a ballroom filled with waltzing couples.

Tchaikovsky's *The Nutcracker* is joined by *Swan Lake* and *Sleeping Beauty Waltz*. Those, along with his *1812 Overture* and *Romeo and Juliet*, are in the All-Time Classical Top 40, and in a lot of people's top 10. *1812* is one of the great "makes you want to get up and move" pieces ever. All of his work, especially *Romeo and Juliet*, is a study in how to explore and develop a theme or two to their fullest.

Here are some other must-hear pieces:

Johann Sebastian Bach's *Toccata and Fugue in D Minor* is, not to put too square a point on it, just extremely pleasant. His *Jesu, Joy of Man's Desiring* is equally so, and one of those that will have you saying, "Oh, *that's* who wrote that" almost the instant you hear it. Bach's *Brandenburg Concertos*.

Beethoven's *Für Elise*.

From the New World, also known as the *New World*

Symphony, is a sweetly moody work by Anton Dvorak (pronounced Dvorjak), a Czech composer who had a reputation
for embracing sternly nationalistic themes, á là Wagner, but
whose best-known composition—this one—was written
while he was visiting the U.S. Also recommended is his *Suite
in E Major.*

Chopin's *Military Polonaise* and *Grande Valse Brilliante*
(Waltz No. 1).

Edvard Grieg's *Piano Concerto Opus 16* is one of the
most famous single pieces of classical music and has been
recorded in pop versions that made the Top-40 charts as
recently as the '70s.

Handel's *Water Music* is, in places, so evocative of water
that you may have to pause the CD to go to the bathroom.

Mendelssohn's *Concerto for Violin* and *Orchestra Opus
No. 64:* If your mind's eye doesn't see nymphs frolicking, or
lambs frolicking, or fawns or children or stockbrokers or
something frolicking, maybe it's time you went in for a mind's
eye exam.

Rimsky-Korsakov's *Scheherazade* is a must, because you
can almost see the scimitars flashing and the samovars gleam-
ing and because it is one of the author's personal favorites.

Rimsky-Korsakov's *Procession of the Nobles* from the
infrequently heard opera *Mlada.*

The Military March from Schubert's *Opus 51.*

An Artist's Life and the Overture to *Die Fledermaus* (The
Bat) by Johann Strauss, Jr.

If It Sounds Familiar . . .

EVEN IF YOU didn't know classical music from hip-hop when you picked up this book, the fact is you've been listening to it—and probably a lot of it—in various forms without even realizing it. Because their copyrights expired long ago, dozens of classical "greats" have been used on TV and radio, in commercials and movies, and as themes for all manner of things for many years. For example:

1930s. *Les Preludes:* One of Franz Liszt's finer tone poems, it was the theme music to the old "Flash Gordon" film serial starring Buster Crabbe (today, he'd probably be making adult flicks) that millions of kids watched in matinees every Saturday.

1940s. Beethoven's *Fifth Symphony:* Specifically, the opening four-note phrase of three quick e-notes, followed by a heavy c-note: dit-dit-dit-DAHHH! As it happened, Morse code was used heavily during World War II, and three shorts and one long were Morse code for the letter V, which stood for Victory. Hence his phrase became the shorthand musical symbol for Victory, much like Churchill flashing the V-sign became the shorthand visual symbol. This was especially ironic, considering Beethoven was German.

1950s. *William Tell Overture:* It's one of the great works of the Classical period, but the American public knows it by its true identity—the theme of "The Lone Ranger." The show always ended with somebody wondering, "Who was that masked man?" but for some reason, nobody ever added, "And who wrote that music that's always playing when he rides off?" The answer: Gioacchino Rossini.

1960s. *Also Sprach Zarathustra:* by Richard Strauss (no relation to the waltz Strausses). It's the music you heard when the earth-sun-moon lineup appeared in *2001: A Space Odyssey,* and since then has become generic, both seriously and satirically, as a kind of standard theme to any momentous event. It had a second 15 minutes of fame in 1972 when the eclectic Brazilian artist Deodato recorded a Top-40 jazz-funk-fusion version with such esteemed jazz musicians as Billy Cobham, Stanley Clarke, and Ron Carter. It would be *the* perfect theme for Viagra TV commercials.

1980s. Pachelbel's *Canon:* It was practically the only pleasant thing about the gloomy and neurotic film *Ordinary People,* in which it was the eight-note refrain, played over and over, each time a bit more ornately and with more complex instrumentation. For many people, it calls to mind rainy days, hearth fires, and therapy.

Here are more "pop classics":

Fanfare by Jean-Joseph Mouret is the opening theme on PBS's *Masterpiece Theatre,* but then, if you watch *Masterpiece Theatre,* you should already know that and, in fact, probably shouldn't need this book. Also, if you're a PBS watcher, you've heard Handel's *Water Music* theming more than one production.

For a number of years, a little slice of Beethoven's *Ninth Symphony* was the theme at the close of the *NBC Nightly News* with Chet Huntley and David Brinkley. If you think that's undignified, a different slice of the Ninth is what everybody sings in that scene with Ringo and the tiger in the Beatles movie *Help*.

In the very same movie, there's a strange kind of "Honey I Shrunk a Beatle" adventure wherein Paul is reduced to the size of a salt shaker and runs around naked on the floor during a general melee. The accompanying music is from Wagner's *Lohengrin*.

Dance of the Hours from Amilcare Ponchielli's opera *La Gioconda*, written in 1876, is a lovely tune, but Allan Sherman changed the libretto (words) somewhat when he recorded his kid's-letter-from-camp parody version in the early '60s, which you no doubt know as "Hello Muddah, Hello Faddah."

The melody of Johann Martini's pleasant love song, *Plaisier d'Amour*, might reside in obscurity today if someone hadn't added the words, "Wise men say, even fools rush in," etc., and Elvis Presley hadn't made it a big mid-1950s hit called "Can't Help Falling In Love."

Strauss's *Blue Danube Waltz* is the music that you hear in *2001: A Space Odyssey* when the rocket from earth docks with the slowly revolving circular space station.

If you liked that strange, alternately manic and portentous music at the end of Woody Allen's *Love and Death*, it happens to be Sergei Prokofiev's *Lieutenant Kije Suite, Opus 60*.

Brahms' *Lullaby* is that "Hush a bye, and good night" music that is virtually synonymous, musically speaking, with bedtime in general and baby's bedtime in particular.

Morning, from Edvard Grieg's *Peer Gynt* suites, is to the dawn what Brahms' *Lullaby* is to bedtime, and has been the background theme for literally hundreds of "sunrise" scenes in films and cartoons.

Tchaikovsky's *1812 Overture* is almost the musical def-

inition of the triumphal march, and if you haven't heard it
used on at least a couple of TV commercials (especially lug-
gage), you must be quick with the Mute button.

Light Cavalry by Franz von Suppé is the all-time classic
fox-hunting or chase-on-horseback music, and kept hundreds of studio musicians working during the age of the cow-
boy movie.

Funeral March of a Marionette by Charles Gounod
(1818–1893) was the theme music of the Alfred Hitchcock
show on TV. Gounod, a French composer of moderately successful operas, probably thought he'd be remembered for his
Faust or *Romeo et Juliette*. Ah well, *c'est la vie.*

The music that is traditionally played at weddings after
the vows, as the happy newlyweds promenade up the aisle,
is "The Wedding March" from Wagner's *Lohengrin,* and if
you haven't heard it several dozen times, it's because your
friends aren't marriage material, or are the kind of neotra-
ditionalists who play *Goin' to the Chapel* instead.

Maurice Ravel is considered an Impressionist period composer, which we said we weren't going to go into, and he
didn't write *Bolero* until 1928, but it is without question an
example of classical music—hey, it's been used as a *ballet,*
for Pete's sake—and the bet is $5 that you know it. Remem-
ber the lovemaking music that Bo Derek played for Dudley
Moore in the movie *10?* You can just mail in the money.

Bach's *Ein feste Burg* doesn't get a lot of airplay on the
classical music stations, but it's an old musical friend and
perennial spiritual hit to millions of regular churchgoers,
who know it as the hymn "A Mighty Fortress Is Our God."

Indeed, if you want to hear a lot of fine classical music
on a regular basis for free, you may just want to get religion,
or at least get thyself to a house of worship. Specifically, a

Protestant house of worship with a traditional-minded music director and a good organist and/or choir, because a considerable body of work, especially by the early 18th-century composers, was religious in nature, and much of it remains popular today in the form of hymns written for the Lutheran and related denominations.

Bach wrote more of these than anybody, the most popular after "Fortress" being the lovely *Jesu, Joy of Man's Desiring.* Others that may ring a bell with you are his "Awake for Night is Flying," "All Together Praise Our God," "O God Our Father, Throned on High," and "Blessed Jesus, at Thy Word."

Mozart and Haydn also produced a number of fine tunes for the sacred sector, and Schumann published an entire book of hymns. But other than Bach, the composer most identified with outstanding religious works is Handel, who, like the Hallmark Company, made a pretty good living just off Christmas alone. Along with the *Messiah,* he also gave us "While Shepherds Watched Their Flock by Night" and one of the two big-name classical compositions that you, or anyone else, are most likely to have actually sung: "Joy to the World." (Ironically, Felix Mendelssohn, who took flak from Wagner for being Jewish, wrote the equally beloved "Hark the Herald Angels Sing.")

Another important composer, Vivaldi, wrote *The Four Seasons,* a classic most people have heard.

And finally, if you're a big cartoon fan, not only do you *really* need this book, but you may already know that parts of Wagner's *Die Walküre* and *Tannhäuser* were what the orchestra played, and Bugs and Elmer sang, in the Warner Brothers Bugs Bunny classic that many animation buffs consider the greatest single cartoon of all time, "What's Opera, Doc?"

Th-thea, th-thea, th-That's All, Folks.

The Pantheon:
The Great Composers

Johann Sebastian Bach (1685–1750)

BY GENERAL ACCLAIM, Bach stands as the greatest composer of the Baroque period, and the one who raised
Baroque to its highest levels. Beyond that, he's considered
one of the most inspired and brilliant composers ever, with
perhaps the most complete mastery of the most musical forms
and instruments of all the greats. He lived most of his life
within a 50-mile radius in Germany, and wasn't fully appre-
ciated as a composer by the general public until almost 100
years after his death. Ironically he was originally renowned
as the greatest solo organist in Europe. Few of his compositions were published during his lifetime, and a lot of his
work was lost, but he was so obsessively prolific—think of
Stephen King with a clavichord—that over 1,000 of his compositions have survived, covering virtually every musical
genre of the time.

Personally, he was stubborn, hot-tempered, touchy, impa-
tient, irritating and generally a pain in the rear; his various
employers especially suffered from Bach-aches. A devout
Lutheran, he created music primarily for the church, yet
fathered 20 children, the most of any major composer that
we know of. Hallelujah.

The Bachs had been professional musicians since the early 1600s, and Johann Sebastian's father upheld that tradition as the town musician of Eisenach, where he played and taught his son the violin. Johann's parents died when he was nine, after which he was raised by an older brother, a professional organist who taught him that instrument.

At age 18 he became the town organist of Arnstadt, where he annoyed his colleagues as a picky perfectionist and fought with the town authorities over his duties and working conditions—basically setting the theme of his professional life. After a few years of menial positions, he became the court musician at Weimar, a major career move. Over nine years there, he produced his first major works, including the *Toccata and Fugue in D Minor* and *Passacaglia*. When Weimar failed to elevate him to the position of Kapellmeister (musical director), he tore up his contract and declared himself a free agent. The Weimar authorities jailed him for 26 days to no avail.

As conductor and composer for the Cöthen court orchestra, he reeled off concertos, sonatas, and solo suites for various instruments, and two of his finest works: *The Brandenburg Concertos* and part one of the *Well-Tempered Clavier*, possibly one of the greatest keyboard pieces ever. After seven years at Cöthen, he went to Leipzig as musical director, where he and the town fathers got along like a bagful of cats, and he created such milestone works as the *St. John* and *St. Matthew Passions* for orchestra and chorus.

Bach was a teacher and an experimenter with music. Some of his best works were originally just complex technical exercises that he transformed into compositions, such as *Art of Fugue,* which was left unfinished at his death in 1750. It's no coincidence that, as is generally accepted, the Baroque period ended the same year.

Toward his last days, the flowery Baroque style was falling from favor. The hot, hip *new* sound was the simpler, more elegant Classical style, and Bach found himself being written off as a musical dinosaur compared to such emerging composers as ... his son, Johann Christian. Johann's older brother, Carl Philipp Emanuel Bach, gained some notoriety in London by working for Frederick the Great in Berlin, and for playing duets with the young Mozart ... sitting on his lap.

Bach is regarded as one of the supreme masters of counterpoint—the interweaving of individual musical threads or themes—and also of harmony. He was the first of the Greats, and you can get a good argument wherever classical is played that he was the greatest, period. Of course, where classical music is played, a good argument mostly involves phrases like "Oh bosh."

Bach's great signature pieces include the *Well-Tempered Clavier,* the *Brandenburg Concertos,* and the *Toccata and Fugue in D Minor.*

Georg Friedrich Handel (1685–1759)

A German by birth, he became so English a composer that they buried him in Westminster Abbey. He even Anglicized his first two names to George Frideric. But whatever handle Handel went by, he was second only to Bach as a Baroque composer, and one of the great crowd-pleasers, musical entrepreneurs, and promoters in classical history. He left a cushy court job in Germany and moved to Italy, where he mastered the Italian opera just as it was becoming the musical vogue in Europe. When that cooled, he returned to Germany to become musical director for the Elector of Hanover. But a visit to London, where they fell in love with his operas, gave him a taste for the big time. He moved there, resolving to be the toast of London music, and got a terrific shove toward that goal when Queen Anne died, making his former boss, the Elector of Hanover, King George I of England. This happy circumstance pretty much set Handel up for life, although he made and lost fortunes in the music business. Having established himself as perhaps *the* opera composer of the Baroque period (he wrote 40 or so), he turned to writing English oratorios based on the Old Testament, in the process composing the oratorio to end all oratorios, the *Messiah*.

He's definitely one classical musician you should know about, but if all these facts are too much for you to Handel, just make a Liszt. (Welcome to the world of music student humor.)

Franz Joseph Haydn (1732–1809)

Haydn—pronounced "Hydin"—is generally recognized as the "Father of the Symphony," and therefore has been known to generations of classical musicians as "Papa Haydn" (which sounds more like what dad's doing when mama's on the warpath). Haydn is credited with working out the proper balance of the various instruments—the trombone and viola are not created equal, etc.—and dividing the instruments into their four major food groups: strings, woodwinds, brass, and percussion. He shares with Mozart the credit for establishing the piano as a classical instrument.

Haydn set the goal of not merely creating a sound, but developing and expanding it in an orderly manner. He took classical music to another level by bringing a logical structure to it, took chamber music—string quartets and the like—from pretty melodies to a means of expression, took the sonata form—which most classical music is based on—

from little more than a rough idea to a refined and established format. Then he took the day off. It was Haydn who largely worked out the sonata formula, and who saw it adopted by classical composers in general.

Haydn wasn't born to musicians, and didn't even really hit stride until his thirties, when he became the musical director for the court of Prince Esterhazy in Austria. The Esterhazy family adored him and supported him lavishly for the rest of his life. However, for that support they wanted entertainment, and lots of it. Haydn's duties included almost everything but gardening: daily chamber music performances and twice-weekly operas and formal concerts, a workload that produced most of his 25 operas, 104 symphonies, 83 string quartets, and other compositions.

Haydn was the most honored, respected, and publicly popular composer of his period—he briefly taught music to Beethoven and instructed Mozart, who became his lifelong admirer. But Haydn's music was straightforward and uncomplicated, and so was he, which is why he never had an Oscar-winning movie made about him. He was generally happy, normal, even-tempered, generous, friendly, monogamous, and hard-working. He wasn't crazy or deaf or hurting for money. Sure, he was the father of the symphony, but that doesn't even get you a Father's Day card.

Haydn's most highly regarded compositions include the *London Symphonies (Nos. 93–104)* and two oratorios, *The Creation* and *The Seasons,* all of them written while in his 60s.

Wolfgang Amadeus Mozart (1756–1791)

If history has ever produced one absolute and undeniable musical genius, it is probably Mozart. Evidently, complete

musical masterpieces simply *occurred* to him, much like, say, a way to rearrange our sock drawer would occur to us. Mozart would compose entire symphonies in his head before even writing them down, and then would write them in one draft, with no revisions. Imagine John Grisham doing this with one of his novels, and you get an idea of just how prodigious a feat this was.

And speaking of "prodigious," it's a word derived from "prodigy," and that's another thing that Mozart was. He was playing the harpsichord by the time he was four, composing minuets by five and was a recognized keyboard virtuoso performing in concert tours at six. He wrote his first symphony at age nine. His first major opera was performed when he was 14, to rave reviews; the pope made him a knight.

He was a brilliant pianist who could play compositions perfectly even when the sheet music was upside-down. He was a phenom throughout Europe before he could shave, and unlike Stevie Wonder, he had no hired press agent.

Mozart was Austrian, born in Salzburg, where his father, Leopold, was court composer and Kapellmeister. Leo knew a star when he saw one, and gave his son music lessons as a toddler. Wolfgang was famous within five years and for his entire life, which was lamentably short. His first serious job was as court organist and concertmaster to the Archbishop of Salzburg, with whom he would have repeated artistic disagreements until taking a hike to Vienna in 1781.

He was a colossal hit in Vienna as a performer and composer, but was inept at court politics and tended to put almost everyone off sooner or later. (Though a flat-out genius at music, Mozart was by all accounts absolutely average in every other area, and in fact was described as socially crude and uncultured—and that was by his admirers. The movie *Amadeus* was an exaggeration, but maybe not by much. He evidently was, if not an idiot savant, at least a kind of doofus savant.)

Certainly he was financially clueless and imprudent, and consequently lived in a kind of genteel poverty, often reduced to taking music teacher jobs and friends' charity despite the fact that he ultimately wrote over 600 musical works including nearly 20 operas, 25 clavier (keyboard) concertos, 12 violin concertos, more than 50 symphonies, and on and on.

Moreover, after his enormously successful opera *The Marriage of Figaro* in 1786, his music began to grow rather too brilliant, to the point that you almost had to be Mozart to understand and appreciate parts of it. Awkward and unsuccessful at almost anything non-musical, Mozart increasingly isolated himself with his composing and dashed off his final three symphonies in less than three weeks in 1788.

Perhaps he sensed that time was short. His health, which even on good days would worry an HMO, was seriously failing. When he was commissioned to write the *Requiem* funeral mass in 1791, he suspected that he was writing it for himself, and he was right: He died on December 5, before completing it. There were rumors that he was poisoned by Antonio Salieri, the envious colleague played by F. Murray Abraham in *Amadeus,* but there was no real evidence, and in Mozart's case poison probably would have been gilding the lily. He was buried in an unmarked grave.

Mozart is as much legend as musician. His ability to write brilliant and virtually complete compositions as fast as his hand could move the pen was, and is, astonishing. Many consider him the finest pure melody writer ever, and the man who basically perfected the classical-era symphony, opera, concerto, and string quartet. Just imagine what he could have accomplished with a full life, good health, and a less goofy name than Wolfgang.

His greatest triumphs were primarily operas, such as *The Marriage of Figaro* (1786), *Don Giovanni* (1787), and *The Magic Flute* (1791). Other outstanding works include the *Jupiter Symphony* and *Eine Kleine Nachtmusik* (A Little Night Music).

Ludwig van Beethoven (1770–1827)

Beethoven is one of the great brooding, reclusive geniuses of all time—his portrait is the very definition of "glowering." Thanks to untold Peanuts cartoons, he's probably got the most recognized mug (sometimes printed *on* a mug) of all the classical composers. Somewhat more importantly, he's

been the central figure in classical music for over 175 years.

He suffered chronic poor health, occasional financial trouble, a miserable love life, and a chaotic childhood, and evidently poured his emotions into his music, based upon which, the man was obviously an emotional goldmine. Or mess. Either way, there's no arguing with the results.

He never married but had a number of relationships with women whom he could never have, especially a mystery woman his love letters addressed as "Immortal Beloved." She was obviously the major romantic figure in his life, because they made that the title of his film biography. Beethoven experts still argue about her identity, but then, what else do Beethoven experts have to do?

The most remarkable aspect of his life is that he gradually went deaf beginning at around age 30, composed a ton of incredible music and never actually heard many of his finest works out loud. In later life, shamed, frustrated, and depressed by his affliction, he became a virtual recluse, and at one point wrote that his music was all that kept him from suicide. In the world of classical music, he is the ultimate tragic figure—and that was even before Hollywood named a Saint Bernard after the poor guy.

Born in Bonn, Germany, he was the son and grandson of musicians and was a semi-prodigy working professionally at age 14. But his mother's death and father's alcoholism

totaled his home life, and in 1790 he left for Vienna, where he lived out the rest of his days. Never much of a "people person," he didn't perform publicly until he was 25, but was an immediate hit with the public and with the aristocracy, whose financial support gave him more freedom to follow his own musical will than most classical composers enjoyed. (Several princes offered him an annual retainer if he just promised not to leave Vienna.) Beethoven was oddly obsessed with Napoleon and wrote several pieces, including a victory symphony, celebrating Napoleon's defeats. Many of these pieces were written in his brother's basement, under cannon fire by the French army. He was also one of the earliest to make serious money from paid public performances and the sales of his sheet music. Financially, he was perhaps the first "bankable" name in music.

He wrote outstanding piano solos, violin sonatas, concertos and chamber music with equal success, but is particularly celebrated as the master of the symphony. His creative pattern was to put an idea down in rough form in his notebooks and then re-work and elaborate and polish it endlessly into a Great Composition. He was a revolutionary for his time, who expanded the size of the orchestra by writing "massive" symphonies, and made the piano a major classical instrument. Students of classical music praise the scope, grandeur, and personal intensity that his compositions convey, and the logic and structure of his music.

During his later years, his deafness grew profound and his music seemed to become more introspective, especially as he cut himself off from the world. But his *Ninth Symphony,* with its *Ode to Joy,* is one of the most renowned and celebratory pieces of classical music ever written.

He was easily one of the most influential composers in

history, and left his imprint on the music of Schubert, Mendelssohn, Wagner, Brahms, and Mahler. His music set the standard for expressiveness, just as he did for artistic triumph over adversity. He remains the most popular and most performed of all the great classical composers 175 years after his death.

Franz Schubert (1797–1828)

Schubert is considered to be the finest pure classical songwriter in history, the absolute master of the melody. He was another prodigy — he wrote three symphonies, a roomful of chamber music, and almost 200 songs by his 19th birthday. And he composed music like somebody had a meter running, writing songs almost as quickly as you could hum them. He produced an absolutely enormous amount of music, including 634 *lieder* alone. (A *lied* is an "art song" that is set to a poem.) He was the first great composer who wasn't also a conductor or concert musician. Or much of anything else. Schubert wrote music, period. In fact, he was sort of a music bum who made modest sums selling his compositions, but largely sponged off his friends. He never left Vienna — he rarely even left his writing desk — and only performed one public concert. To top it all off, his timing was lousy: His only concert took place shortly before he died, at the age of 31. In fact, his life was so short and retiring that he was virtually a professional secret for 40 years after his death, until he was discovered by the world of classical buffs. Now he's regarded as a creative titan. Who knew? Among his most admired works are *Die Schöne Müllerin* (Fair Maid of the Mill), *Die Winterreise* (The Winter's Journey), *Schwanengesang* (Swan Song), his "Unfinished" *Eighth Symphony,* and "Great" *Ninth Symphony.*

Hector Berlioz (1803–1869)

One of the lesser-known names in classical music, Berlioz was enormously influential not so much for his compositions—he only produced a few outstanding ones—but for being the principal shaper of the modern orchestra and one of the great innovators in classical history. He was among the first Romantic period composers and wrote massive, ingeniously orchestrated pieces. He thought nothing of writing for 150 instruments, and once called for 467, plus a chorus of 360 more to keep them from getting lonely. He was a radical who violated the rules with brilliant abandon, and roamed Europe on conducting tours simply to show the world his vision of real music. Because he had very little formal musical training, musical traditionalists blew him off, but he broke acres of ground in expanding the capabilities of the orchestra and experimenting with new meters and harmonies, and influenced many of the century's biggest musical names. In the end, he was known across the continent as the founder of the Music of the Future. His best known work was the *Symphonie Fantastique,* a musical portrayal of the stupefied reveries of an artist whacked out on opium. Makes you wonder how he held onto the pen.

Felix Mendelssohn (1809–1847)

How great Mendelssohn was seems to depend on what generation you live in. He followed Beethoven as the top-gun in classical music in Germany during the 19th century. Then the tide changed, and for years the prevailing view was that he wrote a few exceptionally terrific pieces and a whole lot of grade B throwaway. Now he seems to be returning to high respectability. Whatever, he was a prodigy who out-prodigied even Mozart, debuting publicly as a pianist at age nine and composing serious music at age 11. He was singularly talented across the board—a virtuoso at the piano and violin, an outstanding conductor, and a major composer who launched a revival of Bach's music. But his writing was always too conservative to really capture listeners' imaginations, and sometimes too demanding for musicians to enjoy playing it; his violin concertos made more than one fiddle player just want to throw himself on his bow. Alas, also like Mozart, he died at a ridiculously early age—38—so maybe his best stuff was yet to come. His *Reformation* Symphony and *Hebrides* Overture are particularly well-liked, as is his extremely tasty *St. Paul* oratorio. (And, no, he didn't follow it up with a *Minneapolis* sonata.)

Frederic Chopin (1810–1849)

Whenever the discussion turns to Chopin, the first thing you want to remember is that it's pronounced "Show-pan," not "Choppin'." Chopin wasn't prolific—only about 75 works on record—and he wasn't large-scale—no operas, two piano concertos, three sonatas for piano, and one for cello and piano. Almost everything he wrote was for the piano, and most of that was dance music. He rarely played in public, and never in grand halls, preferring salons and groups of a few hundred invited guests, and only gave three recitals after the age of 26. So how does he get into a book on classical music? Because he was one of the greatest pianists in history, and probably *the* greatest piano composer. In both roles, he was daring, inventive, brilliant, dazzling, and took the whole concept of piano to places no one had even thought of, and we're not talking Cleveland. The **étude** was little more than a practice exercise until Chopin turned it into a minor musical art form. To top it all off, he was self-taught! (Of course, in one sense that means that he learned from the best.) A prodigy, he was composing ditties at age eight, and played his first public concert at 18. He would probably get even more space in this chapter if he hadn't died of tuberculosis at the age of 39. If you're into bar bets, you can make one that more people have wept while listening to his music than to that of any other composer. The hook: His Opus 35 contains the *Marche Funèbre,* more commonly known as the *Funeral March.*

Robert Schumann (1810–1856)

Schumann was best known perhaps as a music critic, and was as much a musical scholar, gadfly, and provocateur as a composer, first beating the drum for new and innovative music through a musical journal that he published, then composing some 150 works, mostly tunes based on character sketches, that became famous not just because Schumann wrote brilliantly but also because he had married brilliantly. His wife, Clara Weick Schumann, was the preeminent female pianist of her time, albeit mostly before and after their marriage, and she played the pants off his songs in tours all across Europe. It worked far better for them than for Ike and Tina Turner, establishing him as the first major anti-Classical classical musician.

Schumann helped bring about the Romantic period by rejecting the notion that form—specifically, the sonata variety—should dominate composing. The *content* of the music, the idea it set out to express, *that* should determine what form the music took. He influenced a number of great 19th-century composers who wound up producing far better Romantic music than he did, but he got the ball rolling. Some people, of course, just wrote him off as nuts—and they had a point, too: He began hearing voices in 1854 after struggling with mental illness most of his adult life, and died in an asylum two years later. Even so, this is the guy who wrote the splendid *Rhenish* Symphony. A lot of today's songwriters should be so nuts.

Franz Liszt (1811–1886)

Liszt is the reason Chopin was not rated *the* finest pianist of his time. Liszt was, in fact, very likely the best ever. He had no competitors; his peers heard him play and just threw up their hands, which were fortunately attached to their arms. Along with being technically astonishing, he was a showboat who obliterated the tradition of the stiff, hunched-over concert pianist. He lurched and swayed, his hands soared and bounded, and his bravura style became the world's. He was the closest thing to a rock star produced by the classical era: Women cried out and fainted at his performances, and so many demanded locks of his hair that he got a dog that he surreptitiously clipped just to satisfy the requests. He was admired as being generous and helpful to other musicians, and perhaps even more admired for his reputation as a ladies' man (if some of the tales were true, we're talking a ladies' superman). A Hungarian, he is primarily known today for the **rhapsody,** which he made into a popular Romantic period genre, especially with his *Hungarian Rhapsodies*. But he is most significant musically for having invented the symphonic poem, or tone poem, a single movement of music which, adapting structures like the sonata form, set out to musically reproduce whatever subject it was based on: a poem, a play, a painting, a particularly successful date, whatever. His new musical form became the rage in Europe. As a composer, he

tended toward the macabre in his themes: His greatest hits were the *Dante Symphony* and the *Faust Symphony*— which stamped him rather literally as a hell of a composer—and the *Totentanz*— which means Dance of Death and lends a rather ugly meaning to the term "cutting in."

Richard Wagner (1813–1883)

A world-class egomaniac, Wagner considered himself God's gift to everyone in general and Germany in particular. By all accounts, he was almost insanely arrogant, vain, self-confident, self-indulgent, unprincipled, bigoted, and shameless, with a personality like a barking dog. But he was also a musical genius, and knew it, and left the world of music different than he found it.

With only minimal musical background, he decided at age 15 that he wanted to be a composer, taught himself how, and was writing minor operas in his 20s. He would become the greatest composer of German opera and a premier composer of opera, period, in the 19th century and even after his death.

His first big hit was *Der Fliegende Holländer* (The Flying Dutchman), which got him appointed conductor in Dresden, where he knocked out subsequent killer operas *Tannhäuser* and *Lohengrin*. But just when things were going along nicely, Wagner, who never met a rash decision that he didn't like, got involved in a movement to overthrow the government. This displeased the government so thoroughly that he had to flee the country to Switzerland for 12 years.

He put the time to good use, developing and writing about his theories of opera as "musical drama," and composing his milestone *Der Ring des Nibelungen* (which most people shorten to "the Ring Cycle") —a series of four operas, including his longest home runs, *Die Walküre* (The Valkyrie) and *Götterdämmerung* (which sounds like something Wagner yelled when the brass played too weakly, but actually means Twilight of the Gods). During this period he also wrote *Tristan und Isolde,* a sort of operatic psychodrama that music scholars have analyzed and dissected over the years the way English Lit majors pick apart *Hamlet.*

Wagner firmly believed in the power of myth and legend and went about creating his own by basing most of his works on heroic German myths and legends, glorifying German arts and warning against the contamination of the noble German spirit by such foreign elements as Jews—he was a raving anti-Semite—and the French—Paris had ignored his early attempt to establish a reputation there, and he never forgave it.

To Wagner, music was the window to the soul, and it was important, even vital, that one's music make this absolutely clear to the listener. Wagner's music frequently made it clear with loud and booming crescendos that could produce high-end hearing loss as efficiently as anything The Who ever did. His compositions were overwhelmingly Teutonic—one might even say too Teutonic—with such a sense of martial enthusiasm that there are parts of *Die Walküre* where you expect the orchestra to rush right out and invade Poland. (Adolf Hitler considered Wagner the model of the Master Race composer, and designated his works as Nazi Germany's official Music to Conquer the World By. Fortunately, Wagner's stuff wasn't *that* powerful.)

Wagner had several extramarital affairs, including one with Liszt's daughter Cosima, whom the composer married after basically finagling her away from her husband. (*See War of the Muses.*)

Wagner was absolutely second to none in his undying respect, admiration, and unqualified love for ... Wagner. He had a remarkable talent for separating royalty and romantically-minded women from their money, and no qualms about using that talent: He stated more than once that the world basically *owed* him whatever it took to support his creative life.

Fortunately for him, a young Bavarian nitwit king named Ludwig tended to agree, and picked up the tab during the last 20 years of Wagner's life. Ludwig eventually went mad (*who* could have guessed?), but not before Wagner convinced him to help underwrite a theater in Bayreuth that Wagner designed and that would be devoted *solely to presenting the works of Wagner,* a vanity that went unsurpassed until the Disney Channel. But it was a brilliant move and made Wagner almost overnight into the McDonald's of European opera, produced in practically every town you visited.

He was the most controversial figure in music in his time, which seems precisely the way he wanted it, with equally large and ardent groups of disciples and detractors. Like Newt Gingrich, people either idolized or despised him, but nobody could deny his talent for raising money and issues.

He created a whole school of musical thought whose core idea was that music should be grand, epic, mythical, inspirational, swollen with emotion, and brimming with life force. In opera, for example, music would no longer support the dramatic action, it would be *part* of the dramatic action. Essentially, you could say the same thing for Wagner.

Jacques Offenbach (1819–1880)

Offenbach was a reasonably important composer whose specialty was comic opera and whose best-known works are *La Vie Parisienne* and *The Tales of Hoffman.* He was not a major figure, and was considered frivolous because his genius was satire, not composing. But he did some very interesting things. For the first few bars of *Barcarolle* in *Hoffman,* the violins sound spookily like a takeoff on the shower scene from *Psycho,* before easing, in a remarkable transition, into a graceful and idyllic melody. Even so, in musical history terms, he was marginal. He is included here mainly because if you don't know about him, the joke on page 112 doesn't work.

Johannes Brahms (1833–1897)

Brahms is important to musical historians because he was the leader of the conservative classical school in the latter 1800s, whose members were artistically opposed to the envelope-stretchers in the Wagner camp. The Wagnerians believed that music should *communicate* some strong image, emotion, or event. Brahms and his fellows believed, not to oversimplify, that music was music—notes and chords and tunes—that should be written as beautifully as possible and then just enjoyed by listening. Traditionalists loved him, and people who found music vexingly complicated *really* loved him. Brahms wrote very few sacred works, none of them specifically for church performance, and most notably the "German" Requiem. His greatness lay in his symphonies, concertos, piano and chamber works.

Peter Ilich Tchaikovsky (1840–1893)

Tchaikovsky's works have probably gotten more young people interested in classical music than any other composer's, but perhaps for that reason, it is musically sophisticated to think of him as a "pop" classicist and not one of the true heavyweight greats. Bah. He wrote some of the most fabulously powerful and romantic music ever. He's one of classical music's most formidable names, especially when you try to spell it. One of the first great Russian composers, he didn't even get serious about music until he was 21, but ultimately turned out an extraordinary string of classical "hits."

Tchaikovsky wrote melodies as if he'd invented the concept and was arguably the best ballet composer of all time, with *Swan Lake, Sleeping Beauty,* and *The Nutcracker* being the cream of the crop. Much of his work incorporated elements of Russian folk music, and certainly incorporated Russian soul. In five minutes, he could go from strains so sweet that you can see why people cry at this stuff, to mighty musical salvos you'd swear were out of *Ben-Hur* or *Victory at Sea.*

His homosexuality, which was a poorly kept secret, caused

him considerable grief, but his music was usually exultant, especially the *1812 Overture.* On the brighter, and odder side, he was financially secure enough to pursue his art thanks to a rich widow who offered to pay him a generous allowance on the sole condition that they never meet, which sounds vaguely like Michael Jackson's marriage. Although they often showed up at the same concerts, they held to the deal for 13 years.

Tchaikovsky's most outstanding pieces include all those mentioned previously plus his *First Piano Concerto* and the romantic *Romeo and Juliet,* which, if he were alive and composing in today's enlightened atmosphere, might very well be the romantic *Romeo and Doug.*

Gioacchino Rossini (1792–1868)
Giuseppe Verdi (1813–1901)
Giacomo Puccini (1858–1943)

These men were fine composers, but for the most part they strictly wrote operas and large choral works. They were very good at it, granted, and quite successful and popular, but they were sort of one-genre wonders, not true musical giants or groundbreakers who changed or influenced music fundamentally, in a seminal way.

Of course, opera aficionados will consider this to be tin-eared blasphemy, a perfectly respectable position, to which one can only reply, "If you're so musically sophisticated, why are you reading this book?"

This book chooses to view these composers as rather like classical music's version of place kickers in football: What they do is legitimate and important, they score a lot, and the best of them belong in the Hall of Fame. But when it gets right down to it, they're not why you're a fan, and they're not the part of the game you like the best.

Having said that, here are the brief essentials just in case that's the way you want to go:

Rossini was a Classical period composer whose most highly regarded work was *The Barber of Seville,* one of the great comic operas, but whose most familiar work is the *William Tell Overture,* surely the greatest masked-man-on-horseback theme.

Verdi composed during the Romantic period, and a big city opera company almost has to forfeit its license if it goes through a season without performing his *Aida, Rigoletto,* or *La Traviata.* He was the titan of the three, and of classical Italian opera, and cranked out a host of compositions both magnificent and incidental, like a kind of 19th-century Neil Simon.

Puccini, who was still kicking around when Frank Sinatra was the rage, is right on the cusp between Classical and Modern, with his three signature works—*Madame Butterfly, La Boheme,* and *Tosca* all being composed within four years of 1900. What his compositions lacked in innovation, which was plenty, they made up for in sheer emotionalism; and to his credit, he gave some of the best roles to women.

A Bouquet of Strausses

The Strauss family of Vienna—father Johann Sr. and sons Johann Jr., Eduard, and Josef—were to popular music 175 years ago what the Jackson family was in the 1980s: You couldn't get away from them. That's because they had glommed onto the first real craze in classical music and made it largely their own. We're talking about the waltz, which Johann Sr. more or less invented, and which wound up being played in every drawing room in Austria.

(Mind you, the waltz was considered so daring and

promiscuous and sinful by traditional elements of society before then that the clergy condemned it and some courts prohibited it. Today, those guardians of decency would take one glance at a typical high school prom and go into immediate cardiac arrest, but to conservatives, the waltz was the gangsta rap of its day.)

The waltz grew out of the *ländler,* a German/Austrian dance, and began showing up on dance floors around 1775. Johann Sr. (1804–1849) was the first to recognize its commercial possibilities and began composing waltzes in the 1820s in partnership with a local orchestra leader named Josef Lanner. Together, they are credited with defining the waltz as we know it. They were immediately successful, which of course meant that they soon bickered and split up. Lanner's career idled, but Strauss wrote about 150 more waltzes, hustled them diligently, made money like he was on the Internet, and told his son Johann Jr. that for God's sake he shouldn't become a musician.

Johann Jr., however, had inherited his father's musical *and* entrepreneurial talents *and* his absolute mastery of the waltz, and studied music secretly, even forming his own orchestra on the sly at age 19. Its popularity soon exceeded that of the hottest orchestra in Vienna: his dad's. Papa caved, and gave Junior his blessing. And Junior ran with it. He became known Europe-wide as the Waltz King and wrote over 400 waltzes for sale and performance, including the most famous one ever: *The Blue Danube Waltz.* (A bit of trivia, which you can occasionally drag out to fake major expertise, is that the actual name of the piece is *By the Beautiful Blue Danube.*) He was also the Bill Graham of 18th-century Europe, with six orchestras going at once, and sheet music selling by the bale. In 1872 he came to the U.S. and was paid $100,000, an absolutely astounding sum at the time, for just 14 performances. He also wrote a number of remarkably good operettas and almost 500 total compositions of various kinds. You could say he waltzed his way to the bank.

His finest waltzes are considered to be the *Blue Danube* and *Tales from the Vienna Woods*. His *Wine, Women, and Song* was not quite in their league, but you've got to love the name, which concisely summed up the high pleasures of life for generations to come. His operetta *Die Fledermaus* (The Bat) is arguably his very best work. It is elegant, stately, and highly danceable. In other words, The Bat is just right for the ball.

Johann Jr.'s brother Josef composed about 280 dances of various types, and Eduard published almost 320. As Johann Jr. grew too busy keeping track of the money to conduct, they both wound up leading his orchestras. But neither was in the league of Johann the elder and younger.

The Killer B's

You may be wondering, "Why do so many of these great composers have last names that begin with B?"

Well, you're certainly not the first. Over a century ago, conductor Hans von Bülow noted the phenomenon, designating Bach, Beethoven, and Brahms as "The Three B's." And that wasn't even counting Berlioz or Bela Bartok (1881–1945).

But it's hard to imagine this as anything other than coincidence. There was no federal program that automatically placed children of B-named parents into accelerated music classes, nor any widespread belief that B-people were somehow more artistically inclined than average.

In fact, three out of 15 or so isn't really that remarkable.

Four of the first 15 U.S. presidents were named James. In the early 1960s, three of the leading home run hitters in baseball were named Mantle, Maris, and Mays. These things happen. Means nothing.

Unless of course, you're one of those reincarnationist-minded folk who suspect that a single, incredibly talented musical soul passed through life three times, first as Bach (1685–1750), then Beethoven (1770–1827), and finally Brahms (1833–1897). In which case your favorite music is probably the *Twilight Zone* theme.

The greatest name in classical music is not even a contest. The winner, by a long shot, is: *Bach*.

A lot of the credit for this goes to Johann Sebastian, but the fact is, there were 64 members of the extended Bach family involved in the classical music profession from 1600 to 1800. Admittedly, the great majority of them were unremarkable and thoroughly forgettable musicians, but even so, the legitimately significant composers named Bach would have filled half a page in the Composers Yellow Pages. There were Johann Sebastian's sons Wilhelm, Carl Philipp, Johann Christian, and Johann Christoph (when it came to the naming of sons, the elder Bach evidently had a bit of George Foreman in him). There was his cousin Johann Ludwig. There were the brothers Johann Christoph (evidently a popular combination) and Johann Michael, who were not directly related to Johann Sebastian, and also *their* nephew Johann Bernard. (If they'd had motels back then, philandering traveling salesmen would probably have signed the register as "Johann Bach.")

Musical families come and go, but even to this day, the Bachs outnumber the Lennons, Jacksons, Osmonds, and Marsalises combined.

Orchestras

NOT ALL CLASSICAL MUSIC is played by an orchestra, nor is it all meant to be. The whole idea behind chamber music, for example, was that it could be played for your guests in a chamber—a room in your house. Of course, if you could afford to hire professional chamber musicians, your house was probably an estate or a mansion and therefore had some pretty big rooms. Still, a lot of great classical music was written for more modest venues, ensembles, and incomes, primarily music featuring four to ten string musicians. Maybe throw in a couple of woodwinds and a keyboard.

But several forms of classical music require and were written for orchestras, and as lovely and memorable as the smaller stuff is, what really gets the listener breathing heavy are those large-ensemble items: the opera, the concerto, and the symphony.

The truth is, if the orchestra didn't exist, these musical forms would have invented it. We know this is the truth because it is essentially what happened.

If the question ever comes up, you can say that the first symphony orchestra was the Gewandhaus Orchestra of Leipzig, Germany, established in 1743, because that's what the *Guinness Book of World Records* says, and they can probably make a good case for it. But history isn't quite that simple, as Napoleon later discovered.

Orchestras

The very first orchestras were just musicians brought together in small groups to provide the musical accompaniment for plays and ballets and operas. Sometimes, however, the audiences liked the music better than the theatrical production itself (and this was *centuries* before *The Capeman*). Over time, the supporting "musical production" acquired its own fans, following, forms, and identity.

Chronologically speaking, the idea of a large musical group that played for the sake of the music alone didn't really start to take hold until the 16th and 17th centuries and, even then, most such groups were essentially bands—brass and percussion—playing at formal ceremonies. The transition to *orchestra* was made as string instruments came on board—which they had by the end of the 1600s—and then gradually became the predominant, core elements of the ensemble, which took a bit longer. By around 1750, "orchestra" still meant two flutes, two oboes, a bassoon or two, a trumpet, four strings, a keyboard instrument, a lute (very ancient pre-guitar instrument), and drums. The orchestra Bach started with in Leipzig had only eight players and never grew larger than 20, with half of them on wind instruments.

The modern orchestra didn't settle into place until Haydn and Mozart got hold of it. Up to that point, orchestras were frequently little more than whatever a city had in the way of talented musicians to call upon, and the town composer accordingly wrote his music with them in mind, bearing in mind their numbers, abilities, and limitations. Some of our most revered pieces of music sound the way they do by necessity: They were written based on what the composer had to work with.

The more renowned and influential certain composers became, the more able they were to get their way. Haydn wrote his early works for orchestras of a mere 12 to 15 players but gradually expanded them to require 35 to 40. Mozart brought the clarinet into the orchestra, and generally beefed up the various instrument groups. Beethoven added even more, especially basses in the woodwind and brass families. By the mid-1800s, the more prominent European orchestras were 50 strong or more, and a succession of musically ambitious creative spirits—Berlioz, Wagner, Strauss, and their ilk—eventually inflated the orchestra to around 100 musicians, which is about what a big-city, world-class ensemble runs today.

Most orchestras, however, are neither big-city nor world-class and the "average" orchestra (although you should never call one that) consists of around 60 musicians, one-half to two-thirds of them on strings.

Having said that, there is no one rigid, absolute "standard" orchestra in terms of which instruments are included and how many of each are required. That is really determined by the musical compositions one intends to play and what the composers have called for in their orchestration. That

may range from as few as 25 or so instruments up to 120. Ideally, what the composer wants, the composer gets, which can even include a few cannons and church bells, as Tchaikovsky calls for in his *1812 Overture*.

Still, there are certain basic requirements that any symphony orchestra worthy of the title should meet, instrument-wise, and since we live at a point in history when the band on the David Letterman show, with three electric guitars out of about nine total musicians, can call itself "The CBS Orchestra," we'd better define our terms.

A *real* orchestra, the kind that you'd expect when you shell out $120 for concert tickets and wear the stiffest clothes you own, will include (but not be limited to) a piccolo, three flutes, three oboes, an English horn, three clarinets, a bass clarinet, three bassoons, a double bassoon, two French horns, four trumpets, three trombones, a tuba, four kettledrums, and other percussion instruments (snare drum, bass drum, cymbals, triangle, xylophone, and so forth), two harps, 18 or so first violins, 15 or so second violins, 12 violas, 10 cellos, and eight double basses. Your scaled-down, 60-person orchestra will consist of approximately two each of flutes, oboes, clarinets, bassoons, trumpets, and trombones, and approximately one-half the strings of the big major-league orchestra.

Here's the standard physical layout of all this hardware, should you want to spot an actual contra bassoon or cello in its natural environment. As viewed from the audience, the strings are in the front rows, arranged from the smallest (and highest-sounding) to the largest (and deepest), going from left to right—violins, violas, cellos, and basses. In the general center, behind the strings, are the keyboards and wood-winds, and behind them, the brass. The deep brass are at the right rear, the kettledrums are center rear, and the percussion items are right or left rear. You've probably already seen the pattern here: The louder it is, the further back it is. It's too bad this isn't the case with relatives at family reunions.

What Is the Finest Orchestra in America?

Gee, could we get a little more subjective, here?

This is like asking somebody to name the finest actor or rock band or wine or take-out pizza in America. You'll get a lot more impassioned opinions than well-thought-out answers.

Unfortunately, there's no universally accepted, objective, mathematically measurable criterion by which to compare and evaluate the major orchestras, such as current going scalpers' ticket prices, or AM radio air plays, or earned run average. One can, however, if one is willing to invite lots of indignant mail, concoct a list of the major contenders based upon the number of commercial recordings that they've released, the length of their musicians' professional careers, and their reputation among the cognoscenti. If one does this honestly, there's a strong likelihood one will come up with the following finalists:

New York Philharmonic Orchestra
Boston Symphony Orchestra
San Francisco Symphony Orchestra
Philadelphia Orchestra
Cleveland Orchestra
Chicago Symphony Orchestra

This will not go down well in Cincinnati, Atlanta, and many other major U.S. population centers, but it's a list that most people who really know their orchestras can live with, and it contains no real surprises, other than, perhaps, that Cleveland, home of the Rock and Roll Hall of Fame, also has one of the country's finer classical ensembles, or that Chicago is aware of classical music at all.

The top three cities are listed in that order mainly on the basis of their conductors, who are just about the best in the country if you don't count Zubin Mehta: Kurt Masur (New York), Seiji Ozawa (Boston), and Michael Tilson Thomas (San Francisco).

But over the long haul New York takes top honors. The New York Philharmonic isn't just the oldest orchestra in the U.S. (founded in 1842), it's also the one with far and away the greatest series of conductors, perhaps of any orchestra anywhere: Gustav Mahler (1909–1911), Arturo Toscanini (1927–1936), Bruno Walter (1947–1949), Leopold Stokowski (1949–1951), Leonard Bernstein (1957–1969), and Zubin Mehta (1978–1992).

Second place, historically, would probably go to the Philadelphia Orchestra, which is one of the outstanding ones in the world and enjoyed probably the longest unbroken reign of all-time-great conductors: Stokowski for the first 26 years (1912–1938), followed by the brilliant Eugene Ormandy for another 42 (1938–1980).

This list does raise a question that eventually occurs to anyone who takes an interest in classical music:

What Does Philharmonic Mean?

You probably assume that it's a vaguely Latin synonym for "magnificent" or "world-class" or "so formal and elegant that they wouldn't even let you sit in the balcony," but in fact, *philharmonic*—which is indeed of Latin extraction— simply means "music loving," or in this context, "a group devoted to music." Put it next to orchestra, and it's more redundant than descriptive. The fact is, you could just as legitimately form a philharmonic bagpipe quartet. (But if your neighbors are well-armed, we'd advise against it.)

Conductors and Semiconductors

ORCHESTRA CONDUCTOR is one of those jobs, like maitre'd and lieutenant governor, that looks so simple that most people figure *they* could probably do it. But unlike the other two, the job of conducting an orchestra is far more complex, strenuous, and time-consuming than you might imagine—although it *does* also mean getting to order people around. The point is that it's not as easy as it looks.

(Indeed, it's not even as *safe* as it looks. The classic example of Jean Baptiste Lully, who fatally injured himself with his own conducting staff, may be extreme, but baton-wielders get so intense in the practice of their craft that they routinely pay the price in pulled muscles, hyperventilation, and other insults to the flesh. In June 1998, for instance, James Conlon, the director of the Paris Opera, was in Cincinnati rehearsing Stravinsky's *Nightingale* and got so worked up that he stabbed himself in the eye with his baton.)

On the most fundamental level, the role of conductor exists because *somebody* has to set the meter and tempo and maintain the rhythm and keep the instruments together and in balance. Getting musicians to cooperate with and do things harmoniously with others is a considerable, often grueling, challenge. If you've ever roomed with a musician, you know this already. For one thing, it's a job that requires two hands.

Specifically, the right hand holds the baton, which it uses

to direct the **time-beat** with an L-shaped motion—up-down, left-right, up-down, left-right—and to indicate the accents by emphasizing certain strokes—*down,* left-right-up, or *down,* right-up. The left hand is used to signal changes in intensity, or emphasize sudden accents, or to tear the conductor's hair when the trombone soloist develops hiccups.

But these are merely the mechanics and barely touch the surface of the job. The conductor is to the music what the director is to the script—he or she brings the written material to life. The musicians play the instruments, but the conductor plays the musicians. The conductor decides how much intensity to put into the music and how to interpret the composer's instructions. The sheet music may say *allegro,* which means "fast," but what does "fast" mean? How fast *is* "fast"? How soft is "soft," and is it a relaxed, pleasant "soft," or a melancholy, weary "soft?" The conductor decides, based on his sense of what the composer had in mind. As many ways as a film director can take the line, "I can't wait to get my hands on you, my love," a conductor can take a 10-second musical stanza, and in both cases, the outcome can range from brilliant to foolish to confusing to trite.

From the first time music was performed by a group, there has been a need for someone to be in charge. At first, the group usually just designated one of the musicians to keep time. Even into the days of Haydn and Mozart, the conductor was often the lead violinist—because at least half the instruments were strings, and it just made sense. Or it was the keyboard player—because he played in single, sharp notes in a rhythm. Sometimes it was both. For a time, orchestras routinely had the piano player keeping time as the conductor, and the violinist directing the players with his bow as the "leader." This worked about as well as two dogs and one bone.

Conductors and Semiconductors

As the music grew more complex, involved ever more instruments, and kept the violinists and pianists busier just playing their parts, things got out of hand. Often, the conductor and leader would be competing for control of the orchestra like it was a trust fund, sometimes even keeping different beats, which they routinely did by waving a roll of paper, banging a staff on the floor, clapping their hands, stamping their feet, or some bewildering combination thereof. Chaos did not make for great music, and a single controlling authority became necessary.

The first conductors other than musicians were usually the composers, first because they were often employed as conductors (or concertmasters) to begin with, and second because by the time of Bach and Haydn, you almost had to be a composer to understand what the orchestra was trying to do, let alone lead and direct it.

The problem here was that conducting required an ability to communicate with and elicit the cooperation of musicians; diplomacy and patience were valuable skills. Alas, while a few composers were also fine conductors, others were more temperamentally suited to some occupation like, say, prison guard or lighthouse keeper. You could scarcely have picked a worse personality than Beethoven's, for instance, for purposes of conducting. Many of our most brilliant composers were frankly too scatterbrained, cranky, or sociopathic to conduct a fire drill, let alone an orchestra.

Clearly, a separate and independent leader of the orchestra was needed. **Johann Friedrich Reichardt** was probably not the very first, but in 1776, he took over the Berlin orchestra as Kapellmeister, booted the pianist out of the conducting role, and directed the orchestra from behind a desk, center stage, clearly illuminated by the footlights. In other words, he was probably the first conductor to look and act like the conductors of today. He was undeniably one of the most innovative.

Other conductors who've contributed to the evolution of the art include:

Ludwig Spohr (1784–1859) was a leading violinist of the early 1800s who, when he took up conducting the Frankfurt Opera, at first led the orchestra by waving his bow, and later used a roll of paper, and finally went with a *baton,* which he may or may not have been the first to use full-time. In any case, he popularized the use of some visible wand-like accessory to keep time for the musicians. *Why this was important:* Before the visual time-beat, orchestra leaders had kept time by banging, tapping, or whacking something (the floor, their music stand, a table) with something else (their foot, a club, a stick) loudly enough for the musicians to hear. Since no known classical music was enhanced by a loud, annoying knocking sound, the baton was a major stride in musical enjoyment.

Carl Maria Friedrich Ernest von Weber (1786–1826) was a prodigy, a pianist, a composer *(Invitation to the Dance),* and the first of the modern conductors. He had the good fortune, given his name, to be all this before people asked you to sign your autograph. He was appointed conductor of opera at Breslau, Germany, at the Hanson-like age of 18. He raised the horn and clarinet to a level of prominence. And he rearranged the orchestra into its current seating plan, with the strings up front and the winds and brass in the rear. Having the softer-sounding instruments closer to the conductor and the louder ones further off enabled the conductor to hear *all* the instruments, and at a more-or-less equal and balanced volume. Put your tubas and trombones up front, and you never really know just what, or even if, the cellos are playing. Weber was also one of the first conductors to have serious and demanding rehearsals, the idea being that it helped to know what you were going to be playing next before you turned the page. He was regarded as brilliant and imaginative in his interpretation of written music. Naturally, he died young—age 40.

Francois-Antoine Habneck put together in the 1830s what critics and historians called the greatest orchestra ever heard up to that time, emphasizing preparation and individual musical talent. He got the entire orchestra, a big one for its day, playing in unison, with skill and precision and clarity, to a degree that floored the audiences. He also helped establish the dominance of the string instruments, with 55 strings out of 86 total players.

Hector Berlioz (1803–1869) is, in the opinion of the experts, one of the handful of mid-1800s titans upon whom all modern conducting is based. Because he came to conducting not as a musician but purely as a composer, he saw the orchestra not from a violinist's or pianist's point of view, but as a whole, and was the first to fully realize what such an ensemble was really capable of. He literally wrote the book on the subject with his definitive *Treatise on Orchestration*. He was a genius at using the various instruments to their best advantage, and anticipated Phil Spector by a century by going for the REALLY BIG SOUND, the goal being to put *life* into the music. He abhorred sloppiness, and thought nothing of subjecting musicians to 25 rehearsals or more. He would instantly dump players who couldn't cut it talent-wise or who engaged in common forms of musical laziness such as "simplification," which simply meant playing only some of the notes. Think of George Patton with perfect pitch.

Felix Mendelssohn (1809–1847) is ranked by a lot of classical scholars as the all-time master of conducting skill and brilliance. He turned Leipzig into the musical center of Germany, and London so adored him you'd have thought he invented ale. He got a bad rap for supposedly initiating "the Mendelssohn tradition" of concentrating the orchestra's rehearsal time on a few key elements and bluffing its way through the rest, but his accuser in this regard was Wagner, who admitted to doing the same thing. Actually, Mendelssohn's contribution was the notion that the conductor should attempt to recognize and emphasize the parts the *composer* would have.

Richard Wagner (1813–1883) may have been the Conductor of the Century. He created an entire school of thought that held that conducting was not about translating sheet music, but about Infusing With Feeling. Wagner's conducting style was in capital letters. He utterly dominated orchestras and propagated the concept of the conductor as primal force and centerpiece. He was an intense musical student and theorist who created a basic philosophy of conducting that still holds sway. He made conducting into a form of both personal and dramatic expression, a vehicle for inspiration. He was the first cult conductor. He was the top baton in Europe. Let's face it, he was—get ready for the pain—a superconductor.

Hans von Bülow (1830–1894) was second only to Wagner in his admiration for Wagner, and indeed made Wagner's music into his life's passion (and for that matter, his wife's passion as well—see page 89). He assembled an orchestra in the town of Meiningen, Germany, that made up for its lack of size—just 48 players—with a precision and iron discipline that brought it recognition as the finest in Europe and a model for all pretenders to the throne. He conducted everything from memory and made his musicians memorize the scores as well, and then play them standing up. He was also the prime mover in the emergence of the flashy, charismatic virtuoso conductor, and was not averse to the occasional showboat gesture; for example, conducting Beethoven's *Funeral March* while wearing black gloves. He was also the first composer to make a recording, in 1890.

Theodore Thomas (1835–1905) was born in Germany but landed in New York at age 10, and therefore is considered the first American in the annals of great conducting. Originally just a violinist, he became a conductor accidentally, filling-in for a sick friend one evening and finding he liked it. In 1862, when American orchestras were rag-tag, amateurish, and only partial approximations of the real thing, Thomas formed his own and put New York on the musical map with his celebrated Irving Hall concerts, then in 1891 dragged the country into the musical major leagues by creating the fabled Chicago Symphony Orchestra, one of the finest in the world.

Gustav Mahler (1860–1911) thought he had more musical knowledge and talent than most composers, perhaps because he was one, and conducted as if God had personally chosen him for the job. He acquired the label "the tyrant" while directing the Vienna Opera, which he browbeat and drilled into a state of near perfection with an arrogant self-confidence that made legions of musicians fantasize about what *they'd* like to do with that baton. He was an obsessive-compulsive who made a systematic study of the possibilities of the orchestra and approached every performance like it was the Normandy Landing. His constant pursuit of the ideal, however ill-mannered, gets him on the All-Time Greats list.

Arturo Toscanini (1867–1957) was the man who took conducting from the personal, emotional, often overwrought and sometimes maniacal exercise that Wagner had made it, and transformed it into a more rational, technical, straightforward art form. To him, the music was the all-important thing, and he took it both seriously and literally. Like von Bülow, he conducted from memory; like Thomas, he got into the conducting game by filling-in in an emergency: As a 19-year-old cellist at the Rio de Janeiro opera house he was pressed into taking the baton, and directed *Aida* completely without sheet music. He became the prototype of the modern-day conductor, his professional career extending from the 1890s into the 1950s, and is considered the greatest conductor of the first half of the 20th century. He was a strict disciplinarian, but his raw brilliance inspired slavish devotion in musicians.

Sir Thomas Beecham (1879–1961) was legendary for his ability to destroy a faulty musician with a handful of words: He once called a trombonist's instrument "that quaint drainage system you are applying to your face." But his usage of harsh *bon mots* was psychological, not dictatorial, and nobody could wring more out of an orchestra.

Leopold Stokowski (1882–1977) was the great showman of the 20th-century conductors, the colorful, self-promoting, charismatic star of the concert who paid as much attention to how he looked to the audience during a performance as he did to the tempo. London born, he became conductor of the Cincinnati Symphony Orchestra in 1909, and brought it national attention with his sheer flamboyance, then took over the Philadelphia Orchestra in 1912, and established it as one of the best on earth by corralling some of the world's finest musicians and crafting a distinctive "Philadelphia sound." With an ego the size of a sousaphone, he made conducting into a performance—showy, vigorous, intense, and dramatic—even having spotlights focused on him for effect. What Babe Ruth brought to baseball, Leopold brought to the classical orchestra: glamour, exhibitionism, and celebrity. To his credit, and the great ire of purists, he also made a point of exposing audiences to the works of new, lesser-known, and overlooked composers.

Leonard Bernstein (1918–1990) was the first great American conductor who was actually born in America, and to many who've followed him, the first true American conductor, period. He was definitely the first American director and conductor of a globally renowned orchestra (the New York Philharmonic), and the first television-era conductor, who used that medium to bring classical music to the general public in an unprecedented way, and to convince them to enjoy it. (His *Young People's Concerts,* a collection of his television discussions of classical music, is one of the best plain-talk books on the subject available.) He regarded conducting as a performance, and threw himself into the role with the passionate energy of a silent movie actor. He was also a major composer in his own right (*West Side Story* and other Broadway musicals), a superb pianist, and generally a classical music renaissance man. Egotistical, visionary, inspiring, controversial, and overpublicized, a decade after his death he remains the most important classical figure of our times, and maybe the reason you're reading this book.

Robert Shaw (1916–1999) is perhaps the man most responsible for raising the status of American choral singing in the 20th century. Born in the river town of Red Bluff, California, to an evangelist clergyman and his wife, Shaw combined a reverence for the chorale classics with an appreciation of the American musical spirit. Shaw owed much of his success as a choral director to his concept of an ensemble of voices as a single instrument. He reportedly invested large sums of his own money for the pure gratification of exposing music lovers to their first encounter with the choral classics. From 1960 to 1988 Shaw was music director of the Atlanta Symphony Orchestra. Thanks to his symphony recordings, he remains a prominent figure in classical and choral music.

Zubin Mehta (1936–) was born in Bombay to a father who was director of the Bombay Symphony and who clearly intended that Zubin follow in his footsteps. Under dad's tutelage, he won the first International Conductors Competition at age 22 and four years later became musical director of the Los Angeles Philharmonic, which he spent 15 years elevating to a level of international prestige—a feat on the order of performing Shakespeare with the cast of *The Drew Carey Show*. He went on to conduct the New York Philharmonic from 1978 to 1992, and was named the Israel Philharmonic's director for life in 1981, which sounds like a title you get in North Korea, but which hasn't stopped him from roaming the globe as a standing-room-only guest conductor. His emotional and enthusiastic style gets especially outstanding results with Romantic period material.

Seiji Ozawa (1935–) was born in Shenyang, China, and although Japanese, has become so identified as a towering American talent that his status as the first great Asian conductor of western classical music is often lost amid the accolades. After breaking in with the New York Philharmonic in 1961, he went on to conduct a virtual All-Star team of great orchestras, including those of Berlin, Vienna, London, San Francisco, Chicago, Toronto, and La Scala in Milan. A meticulous technician known for his precision and sensitivity, he reigned as the musical director of the Boston Symphony Orchestra for a record 27 years, elevating it to rarefied heights in the Classical standings. The French gave him their Legion of Honor.

The Instruments

THE INSTRUMENTS in the orchestra fall into five families, both in terms of how they are constructed and played, and how they are located in the orchestra.

Woodwinds: So called because they originally were—and commonly still are—made of wood, and blown through to create sound. (Sometimes things *are* as straightforward as they seem.)

   Piccolo. Prehistoric in origin, this may be the first "instrument" ever crafted by homo sapiens, since it's basically just a wooden, or more recently platinum, tube with several holes running along one side, but its first documented use in an orchestra was in 1717 in Handel's *Water Music*. It has the highest note range of any woodwind, which somewhat limits its use by composers, but if you were thinking of taking up an instrument to join a marching band, it's certainly one of the lightest and easiest to carry. It's played sideways sort of like eating corn on the cob, except you don't nibble, you blow across a hole in the side. You might think of it as a little flute, especially since piccolo is Italian for "little flute."

   Flute. It probably goes back as far as the piccolo, from which it differs primarily in size (bigger) and range (lower). Its first known orchestral appearance was in operas around 1672. Like the piccolo, but unlike the other woodwinds, it is played sideways across the body, with the musician blowing not into a mouthpiece, but a hole in the side toward one end.

Oboe. The oboe is the next step up in size, and lower in tone, than the flute. It has a fairly narrow range. It was introduced into orchestral service around 1660 but is considered much younger than the flute overall, dating just to the Middle Ages. The oboe is about a yard long, black and covered with winding shiny keys. To the untrained eye, the oboe may not look much different from a clarinet. The trained eye, however, can see that the oboe has a conspicuously smaller mouthpiece (the size and shape of a straw), and that the bell (the opening where the music comes out) is narrower. Technically, the oboe is a *double-reed* woodwind, meaning that the player blows through a hole between two small reeds. In an orchestra, the oboes are usually found between the flutes and bassoons, in an area you may like to think of as the Oboe Jungle (as long as you don't tell anyone you got the idea here).

English horn. This is a sort of industrial-size oboe with a bulb-shaped bell and distinct sound that gets a lot of solo usage. In range, it's an octave lower than the clarinets.

Bassoon. No, this is not a member of the ape family, nor is it a balloon-shaped fish. Rather it is the long black woodwind that looks like a shipping tube for pool cues, without all the metallic filigree of the oboes and flutes. The bassoon dates back to around 1540 and began popping up in orchestras in the early 1700s, especially after Vivaldi took a serious shine to it. It has the lowest range of the double-reed woodwinds.

Double bassoon (or contra bassoon). Not surprisingly, what we said about the bassoon goes double for this, which is not two bassoons strapped together (or a Latin American paramilitary bassoon), but a sort of bass bassoon, with the lowest range of any standard orchestral breath-powered instrument including the tuba, a fact which is not musically significant but could win you a bar bet or two during intermission. Soundwise, it is the woodwind equivalent of a sumo wrestler. Heftwise, it's the only blown instrument that isn't held, but rests on a base on the floor.

Clarinet. The clarinet was invented in the 1690s, and was first used orchestrally by Vivaldi in 1716. It is one of the most versatile instruments in the orchestra. Its range is both wider and lower than that of the oboe, and it is visually distinguished from the oboe by its mouthpiece, which is more cigar-sized (but don't inhale!), and by the bell, which is more flared out and funnel-shaped. The clarinet is a *single-reed* woodwind. There are several types of clarinets, varying by range of sound. The **bass clarinet** is often added to the standard orchestra.

Saxophone. Now we're into what, in classical terms, amounts to modern technology. Rather than slowly evolving from some crude, prehistoric form, the sax was invented *by* Sax. Specifically, Adolphe Sax, in 1840. It comes in a dizzying array of sizes and ranges that the composer can use to elicit a variety of musical expressions, and the occasional presidential candidate can use to hustle votes on MTV. To be honest, it is not routinely part of the symphony orchestra, but it is fun to write about.

The Brass: Along with allowing record reviewers to get annoyingly cute ("kicked some brass," "sat on his brass," "the head of the brass," etc.), the brass instruments—known more commonly as "the horn section"—are among the very oldest instrument types in the classical orchestra.

Trumpet. Its roots go deep into prehistory, to the first hunter-gatherer who ever thought to blow into a ram's or sheep's horn, and discovered that he (1) made a noise like you wouldn't believe, and (2) instantly got the attention of everyone in the vicinity. The earliest handcrafted trumpets were used for signaling purposes in general, and battlefield signaling in particular, where buglers played such primeval hit tunes as "Charge!" and "Run away!" The Biblical story of the fall of Jericho is one example, and the first recorded instance of a brass section bringing down the house. The trumpet was a staple of the earliest orchestras, especially after the instrument's range and versatility were enhanced by the addition of keys, allowing for the hitting of specific notes, around 1796. The trumpet's range is just a bit higher than that of the tenor sax. Basically, it's a long brass pipe bent into the shape of a big paper clip, with a mouthpiece at one end and a funnel-shaped opening at the other.

Trombone. Before keys came along to make the trumpet a jack-of-all-notes instrument, the ability to play a variety of notes in an orderly and predictable fashion was provided by the sliding part of the trombone, an innovation that dates to the 14th century. First used in orchestras about 300 years later, it also comes in alto, tenor, and bass versions.

French horn. Where the trumpet and trombone are rectangular in shape, the horn's piping is circular and mazelike. It has a softer, richer tone that actually falls midway between the other brasses and the woodwinds. It goes back to Biblical times, and became a regular orchestra member in the latter 1700s.

Tuba. The largest of the brass instruments, it's as much worn by the musician as it is played. The orchestral tuba is significantly smaller than the huge version with the yard-wide mouth that they carry at the end of marching bands and make you glad *you* don't have to play, but it's still a handful. Think of the tuba as the Saint Bernard of brass instruments. It was invented around 1829 to fill the apparent need at the time for a good *oom-pah* sound, or to convey the image of an elephant with indigestion. Berlioz, a composer with definite pluck, was the first to use it orchestrally in his *Symphonie Fantastique* in 1830. It has the same approximate range as a bass saxophone (or for that matter, a foghorn).

Strings: These basically make the difference between an orchestra and a marching band, and they, along with the wind instruments, add such crucial currents as romance, poignancy, sweetness, and melancholy to the orchestra's emotional reservoir. It is no coincidence that when something engages our sense of sympathy or involves us emotionally, we say that it "tugs at our heart strings"—as opposed to saying, for example, that it "warms our heart's spit-valve." Another major difference between the blown instruments and the strings is that the winds and brass come in a variety of designs and construction materials, while almost all the strings are merely larger or smaller versions of a single basic wooden instrument. And the orchestra's string section is one area of life where, incontestably, size matters. The bigger the instrument, the lower the voice. (Bear in mind that this tells you absolutely nothing about the musicians.)

Violin. The violin is the smallest of the major strings. In an orchestra, there are First Violins, which play the main melody, and Second Violins, which play a different, harmonizing melody. The violin descended from the lyre around the 1st century B.C., evolving from something with strings that you strummed or plucked, to something with strings that you rubbed with a bow in order to produce drawn-out notes. It evolved gradually thereafter, and didn't settle into its modern form until 1505 or so. It is thought of as an Italian instrument, partly because the finest classical-era violins were crafted by Italians, most notably Antonio Stradivari (1644–1737), whose Stradivarius violins are as cherished and valuable as any musical instruments on the planet. The violin's first orchestral use was in the early 1500s, and it soon became the mainstay string instrument. Its range falls roughly between those of the piccolo and the flute. And here's a bit of trivia that will get you stared at by almost anyone who hears it: The word "violin" possibly derives from the Latin *vitulari,* which means, among other things, "to skip like a calf." No bull.

Viola. A bit larger than the violin, but otherwise essentially the same instrument, and also played under the chin. Its development was similar to that of the violin. In the early 1500s, before these things were decided, it was a serious competitor for the title of Top String with its smaller brother, the ultimate winner. The viola's range corresponds to that of the alto sax.

Cello. Considerably bigger, and lower in range, it developed alongside the violin and viola, and was, unfortunately for cellists with no sense of humor, given its name many years before the advent of the popular gelatin dessert. Too large to be held for long, it sits on a pointed stand on the floor, the musician seated behind it.

Bass violin. The biggest of the line—it's as tall as a man, and in fact you play it standing up—and the deepest-voiced, and although it's pronounced "base," its name fairly invites lame puns and dumb jokes involving music and fish. (The bass violin: It's great for doing the *scales,* and it definitely has al*lure*.) It has a mellow, throaty sound.

Harp. The grandfather of the string instruments, it easily predates anything that requires a bow. It's prehistoric in origin—the ancient Egyptians not only played it, but inherited it from prior cultures, possibly in the Middle East, where it appeared as long ago as 1200 B.C. It was part of the very first orchestras.

Percussion: These are items that you bang, tap, shake, jangle, jiggle, brush, thump, or slap to produce a beat to the music, or an orchestral special effect such as a ding, clang, crash, or boom. Percussion instruments basically break down into (1) drums, and (2) the other stuff.

Drums. There are more kinds of drum than you could shake a stick at, let alone hit with one, but the three mainstays are the **snare** drum, whose origins go way back to the earliest military forces (the snares are the wires across the

drum's bottom surface that give it that sort of raspy sound), the **kettle** drum (a.k.a. the **timpani**), also of ancient lineage, and originally the size and shape of (surprise!) a kettle, and the **bass** drum, which is of ancient Turkish birth and is the size of a small wading pool. The snare provides the *rat-a-tat-tat* or *brrrrrrr* sound, the kettle the chesty *pom-pom* and the bass the big *boom boom*. The snare and bass were charter members of the orchestra; the kettle joined in around 1607.

Other stuff. The **xylophone** is a sort of half-breed: a percussion instrument that produces musical notes. But it doesn't provide melody so much as occasionally liven or lighten things up. Beyond that, "percussion" mostly boils down to the **triangle,** a small triangular metal bar that is struck to produce a "ding" sound, and a variety of **cymbals,** which produce your basic metallic crashing sound and lots of angry yelling and banging from your neighbors if you practice at home.

Keyboards: Technically, these are all percussion instruments, since you strike the keys to produce the sound. But we're giving them their own category because, frankly, they're too important not to. The **piano** often seems like the president of the instruments—the star and centerpiece of whatever is being played—but the fact is, the keyboards are the most recent additions to the orchestral lineup. The piano only began appearing in orchestras in the late 1700s, and wasn't really perfected until the development of the iron frame in 1859.

Prior to the piano, the reigning keyboards were the **clavichord,** a rectangular box in which strings are struck with little hammers when you hit the keys, and the **harpsichord,** a square or triangular box in which strings are plucked with quills when you hit the keys. Though still used by orchestras specializing in early music and period instruments, both "chords" peaked in popularity in the 1700s, and have since gone the way of the buggy. If either of them is featured in a piece of classical music, it's Baroque period material.

The harpsichord's notes were sharper and clearer, but unvarying in tone and volume. You could get expressive with the clavichord's tone and volume, but the notes were faint and muted. The piano, invented in Florence in 1709 by a harpsichord maker named Bartolomeo Cristofori, combined the positive attributes of both, and ultimately blew them into musical oblivion. Thanks to Mozart and Haydn—the first major composers to embrace the piano—and later Chopin, Schumann, and Liszt, the piano evolved into the star quality instrument of the classical orchestra.

The **organ** is a descendant of another instrument that traces from antiquity: the pipes. In the modern orchestra, however, it's become a bit player. (Which is not to say that the organist has become a *bitter* player.)

Auxiliary instruments: These aren't on the basic orchestra roster, but are brought in from time to time as individual compositions require. Among those that pop up most frequently are the **alto flute, guitar, mandolin,** and **euphonium** (a sort of tenor tuba, introduced in 1840). This category also includes wind instruments invented by people with marvelous names, such as the **Flügelhorn** and the **Heckelphone.** (Presumably, you can heckle a Heckelphonist, but when it comes to a Flügelhorner, just forget what you're thinking right now.) The auxiliary ranks also include a whole host of percussion and/or keyboard items, most commonly the **castanets, glockenspiel, bells, tambourine, gong, marimba,** and **temple blocks.**

Concerted Efforts: How to Enjoy the Live Performance

HERE ARE A few tips that may help you enjoy the live concert to its fullest, or at least more fully than if you completely ignored them.

Try to get good seats. Since concert halls come in all shapes and sizes, it's impossible to generalize as to where the best seats are for listening. In a typical concert hall, the best seats are one-third to one-half way back from the orchestra, in the center, but each hall has its own unique and varying acoustics, and your aural mileage may vary. One rule obtains in every venue. *Don't* take a seat under an overhang or balcony.

Here's an idea: If your local newspaper has someone who writes reviews of classical concerts, call that person at the paper and ask advice on where to sit. Classical music reviewers as a rule are not besieged by people wanting their advice, aid, and wisdom, so there's a good chance you'll get a straight and helpful answer.

Failing that, you may simply have to fall back on the Golden Rule of the musical performance business: The better the seats, the more they tend to charge for them. (Or: You get what you pay for.) Of course, if it's a really world-class venue, you may be lucky to get seats at all, in which case, don't be picky.

There are also pre-concert lectures and read-before-you-go program notes so that you can familiarize yourself with the concert and enjoy the many subtleties. You don't want to be surprised when Romeo dies at the end, do you?

Other tips:

To get the most out of the music, you'll want to be alert. Therefore, try to achieve that perfect coffee level: Enough to keep you awake, but not enough to keep you running to the john.

Incidentally, this is not a baseball game, so you will not be permitted to bring your own food and beverages. Snuff, however, can be a rather suave touch.

If the orchestra seems discordant, confused, out of synch, and unharmonious at first, relax. There's a simple explanation. You've arrived a few minutes early, and what the musicians are doing is technically called "tuning up."

It is considered rude to whistle or cheer, take phone calls, *make* phone calls, do bird calls, call out requests, clap or snap your fingers in time to the music, make that tasteless noise with your hand in your armpit, read (let alone rustle) the newspaper, and keep asking those seated around you, "When's the movie start?"

Don't cough loudly or more than three times without leaving the hall; don't unwrap cellophaned candies or rattle your jewelry.

Wear clean socks in case the urge strikes you to take off your shoes.

Under no circumstances should you whip out your harmonica and join in.

Listening: More Than Having
Two Ears and a Pulse

"Classical music is better than it sounds."
—Mark Twain

T HERE ARE NO hard and fast rules about how to listen to classical music—the basic idea is to *enjoy* it, after all, and not to dissect it and think it to death. But the purists insist that the more you know about and *understand* classical music, the more you *do* enjoy it, and they may be right.

Begin with the fact that the composer is trying to *express an idea* with the music. Try to think of classical music as a form of communication that uses notes, chords, and melodies instead of words, phrases, and gestures. Your assignment as the listener is to hear what the composer is saying. By "hearing" the music, we mean listening to it deliberately, consciously, closely, and even intently.

The music means something, and the conductor and performers are trying to capture that meaning and share it with you. They're wasting their time if you're not paying attention. And, by the same token, you're more likely to really enjoy the music if you're not also painting the kitchen, or reading a spy novel, or driving the kids to the mall, or doing your taxes. (If anybody ever writes music that makes doing your taxes enjoyable, people will start building shrines to the composer.)

The point is, to really *hear* what the music is saying, you need to be aware of what you're listening to. What is the *mood* conveyed by the music? Is it frisky, or sullen? Urgent, or meandering? Pompous, or restrained?

What images does the music call to mind? A romantic interlude? Frantic chase? Sunny glade? Bitter disappointment? Army on the move? Baby ducklings? Baby ducklings *à l'orange?* The clown at your third birthday party? The clowns at your 23rd birthday party?

Does it take a basic theme and put it through some emotional paces—say, lively at first, then languid, then eager, then morose, and so forth?

Listen for *patterns* in the music, for a sense of structure, for melodies that recur in different—sometimes *way* different—volumes and tempos and combinations of instruments.

Try to get a fix on the opening theme and then follow it as the composer develops it, alters its appearance, dresses it up, changes its hair color, and otherwise toys with it, then see how quickly you can spot it again in its original form at the end. (Yes, it sounds complicated, but the Beach Boys' *Good Vibrations* was complicated, and you had no trouble with that.)

No points are awarded for all this, just the heady satisfaction that you may have an actual clue as to what's going on. (Note: If this epiphany should strike while you're attending a concert, remember, no crying out "Aha!" or "Got it!")

To do this right, classical devotees say you should listen to a piece of music more than once, and even repeatedly. This is a good idea, because with repetition, you will either: (1) get sick of it, which means it wasn't really speaking to you to begin with and you can ditch it and move on, or (2) like it more and more, which means it does have some message for you, and, if you listen, you might hear what it is. For example, try listening just to the strings one time through, then only the brass, or the woodwinds, and then all at once, to get a clearer fix on how the composer blends and weaves them together.

Don't get edgy about the idea of repeated listenings. Don't start thinking, "There goes whole chunks of my life, trying to figure out all these huge symphonies and stuff." The fact is, most classical music does not drag on for any serious length of time. Sure, you've got scores that run 45 minutes and more, but many of the very best pieces, such as preludes and overtures, are over before you know it, and even some major works like Beethoven's *Fifth Symphony* only run about 30 minutes. If you can sit through an entire CD of Alanis Morrisette or Fleetwood Mac, Bach and Mozart will be a cruise.

Here's a tip: Try to recognize *yourself* in the music (and no, that doesn't mean that the kettle drum reminds you that your butt seems to be getting bigger). Does it feel the way *you* sometimes feel? Can you hear your own idea of passion, or despair, or celebration, or nostalgia? Does it convey your notion of peacefulness, or enthusiasm, or loss? Is it glad to be alive? Does it enjoy jogging? Does it own a dog? Is it riddled with anxiety over the rising electric bills? Delighted that its annoying co-worker was denied a promotion? Obsessed with how lousy its golf game has been lately?

Maybe you're recognizing more of yourself than the composer intended. But that's okay! To a great extent, classical music is what you make it. And the fundamental idea is to make it pleasant.

Even if you never figure out the music's message or the structural nature of the fugue and sonata, classical music can still be a marvelous way for you to kill time. And after all, isn't that what art appreciation is all about?

Here is a list of other resources that allow you to get inside the head of various composers.

Lectures and Essays: Harvard University sponsors an annual symposium called the Charles Elliot Norton lectures. Some of the greatest musical minds of our century have contributed lectures and essays. These six compose our "greatest hits list":

Poetics of Music; Igor Stravinsky (1939–1940)
A Composer's World; Paul Hindemith (1949–1950)
Musical Thought; Carlos Chavez (1958–1959)
The Unanswered Question; Leonard Bernstein (1973)
I–IV; John Cage (1988–1989)
Concerto Conversations; Joseph Kerman (1997–1998)

Books:
What to Listen for in Music, Aaron Copland, McGraw Hill (1988)
The Joy of Music, Leonard Bernstein, Simon and Schuster (1962)

Videos:
Leonard Bernstein's Young People's Concerts: With the New York Philharmonic, Video Music Education, Inc. (1993)
Marsalis on Music: Sousa to Satchmo, Sony Classical Film & Video Production (1996)

Two's Company,
Eight Hundred's an Audience

A T THIS POINT, you're probably asking, "What is the best *form* in which to listen to classical music: A live concert or a CD? Or what about vinyl or tape?"

Okay, maybe you're actually asking "Why did I ever start reading this book?" Frankly, we can't answer that. But as to the first question ... well, we can't really give you a definitive answer on that one, either. Only you can.

The experts are unanimous that all classical music is better heard live. And indeed, a live performance should always be better than recorded, for the simple reason that you're *there*. You're in the actual presence of the music. The richness, the nuances, the subtleties and qualities of sound that the pros call *texture,* are available to your senses with no intermediary. Plus you can see the musicians playing, which adds to the music. Maybe not as much as a rock concert, of course—nobody's wearing neon eyeglasses or detonating fireworks or biting the head off an iguana, but there's still a lot of visual energy and body language to underscore the music.

Perhaps more important, you're part of a group experience and invariably pick up on the audience's focus, energy, mood, and response. In basketball, the crowd is called the sixth player. Here, the crowd is like an additional, and extremely large, instrument. If everybody around you is awash with sympathy, or anticipation, or jubilation, you feel it. (If they're not awash at all, you can smell it, but that's rarely a problem at your local philharmonic.)

Unfortunately, it's not all upside. With the group experience, you also get the group, especially when it's in line to the beverage bar or the restroom or all hitting the parking lot at the same time. The live concert also involves such music enhancements as those dress shoes that feel like interrogation aids, that seat that somebody in the airline industry must have designed, and the guy sitting behind you who evidently dined on onions sauteed in fuel oil before the concert.

We're talking *atmosphere* here. Admittedly, Bach and Mozart and Chopin and Tchaikovsky didn't write their music to be listened to over a $2,000 sound system while relaxing in a hot tub with a supply of fine chardonnay and a charming companion, but that's probably only because they weren't able to. There's also a lot to be said for classical music by a roaring fire, or drifting on an open bay in a sailboat, or hiking in the redwoods, or *whenever you would really enjoy hearing some classical music.*

With any live performance, you're taking a chance: the orchestra could have an off night, the conductor could be tired, the bassoon player could throw a *grand mal* seizure, or the whole shebang could just be not that good. Nothing against the orchestras and conductors of whatever fine town or city you live in, but it's highly unlikely they can match the London Royal Philharmonic under the baton of Zubin Mehta on its best of five or six recorded run-throughs. Whatever the recording, it will be of a top-flight performance by a top-flight orchestra and leader.

As for CD versus vinyl versus tape, everybody who really

cares already has an ingrained opinion on this matter. In the considered opinion of classical aficionados, CDs reproduce the music with the highest degree of accuracy.

There are also specific drawbacks to both vinyl—that it's impossible to find—and to tape cassettes—that classical compositions were not written to run a neat 15 or 20 or 25 minutes per side, which means that you routinely get a Side A with a 40-minute symphony and a Side B with about 17 minutes worth of concertos and 23 minutes worth of silence that you have to fast-forward through to the end.

Wars of the Muses and
Other Hard Luck Stories

THERE REALLY WEREN'T MANY FEUDS worth discussing between major classical figures. There was plenty of mutual disdain and disagreement to go around, but little overt hostility, and, sorry to say, no duels. Even Wagner, who considered music the stuff of life, and Brahms, who regarded it as notes on paper, may have detested each other philosophically, but they didn't get their knickers all in a bunch over it.

To be sure, some of the *conductors* didn't get along—Toscanini had no use for Mahler, for example—but by and large, the composers were on good terms with one another, and often lifelong friends—Mozart and Haydn, Schumann and Brahms, and so on—or even in-laws, like Wagner and Liszt. The major ongoing feud in the history of classical music is not the Wagnerites versus the Brahmsians or the strict sonata form disciples versus the free form advocates, but probably the trumpet players versus the violinists in any given orchestra.

Still, the annals of classical music have their fair share of scandal, intrigue, shamelessness, and weirdness.

As depicted in the film *Amadeus,* **Mozart** was almost obsessively envied by rival Salieri (1750–1825), to the point that there was considerable suspicion after Mozart's early demise that Salieri had poisoned him. While there was some evidence to that effect, nothing was ever proven, and God knows they couldn't have convicted him in L.A., but that didn't stop Nikolai Rimsky-Korsakov from writing an opera, *Mozart and Salieri,* that basically accused Salieri of whacking Wolfgang.

In a sort of sequel to this scandal, Salieri himself died in the grip of dementia after years of mental deterioration, and some believe he was driven nuts by all the rumors of his guilt.

Schumann probably never poisoned a soul, but nevertheless displayed signs of mental instability as early as his 20s, was driven to attempt suicide in 1854, and died in an asylum. His mental state may not have been helped by the fact that Brahms, his dearest lifelong friend, was also apparently his wife's dearest lifelong friend. The details remain unknown, but the three lived together for several years, and Brahms, who wrote passionately of his love for Frau Schumann, never took a wife of his own. It might be relevant that, at age 13, Brahms practiced piano by playing professionally in taverns and brothels. As the twig is bent.

When Johann Strauss Sr. and Josef Lanner formed the orchestra that probably gave birth to the modern waltz, Strauss was the conductor and Lanner the composer. But then Strauss began composing, and they had a falling out because, said the Vienna insiders, Lanner was ripping off Strauss's superior compositions and putting his name to them. Whatever the truth, the final break came when they actually duked it out at a concert. After that, well, Lanner's music was very nice, thank you—but it was Strauss's stuff that you could *dance* to. Fame and fortune-wise, it wasn't even a contest.

(Josef and Johann Jr., the sons of "The Waltz King," were sort of the Waltz Princes, and wrote a number of them on their own. Sometimes the kids would just sign a composition "Strauss" and leave people to guess and wonder *which* Strauss had done the composing. Not especially scandalous, perhaps, but certainly irritating to music historians.)

Tchaikovsky was gay at a time when the *last* thing that meant was colorful parades and coming out. Deeply closeted and just as deeply tormented by his sexuality, he had relationships with several young men but entered into a "cosmetic" marriage with, unfortunately, an earnestly heterosexual young lady, a short-lived disaster that drove him to attempt suicide by diving into the river hoping to die from pneumonia. The couple separated after nine weeks but never divorced, and Mrs. Tchaikovsky ultimately died in an insane asylum. Tchaikovsky's official cause of death is due to cholera from drinking fouled water, but some Tchaikovsky students believe that he took his own life, possibly with arsenic, to end an affair with a young nobleman. He was almost certainly not the first great homosexual composer, but he's the first whose sexuality we're aware of.

By contrast, Liszt was allegedly as straight—and energetically so—as a rooster, with a reputation worthy of Don Juan, or maybe even Mick Jagger; the barely-biographical film *Lisztomania* depicted him as a kind of frock-coated 18th-century rock star. Franz had a number of flings with members of European royalty and three children out of wedlock with the Countess d'Agoult alone.

Wagner, who was a scant two years younger than his pal Liszt, ran off with good buddy Franz's daughter Cosima, who was not the prematurely plucked flower you might assume she was. As the story goes, Wagner wanted Cosima in the worst way, which is pretty much how he got her. His problem was that she was already married, to conductor von

Bülow. His solution was that von Bülow revered Wagner, and Wagner knew it, and knew that von Bülow would jump like a trained flea if Wagner invited him to come to Munich and conduct the Court Opera, which he did. Wagner and Cosima began having an affair almost before the train came to a full halt. They ultimately had a child, eloped, and reduced von Bülow to the status of Most Celebrated Cuckold in Europe. On the upside, at least Woody Allen wasn't involved. Their love triangle was, for its day, a scandal of "Hard Copy" proportions. If you recall the 1960s Eddie Fisher–Liz Taylor–Richard Burton affair, and what a national buzz it made, just think of this as *Cleopatra* with sonatas and powdered wigs. Wagner, whom almost nobody associates with a genial sense of humor, thereafter enjoyed referring to his friend Franz as "papa." How Franz in turn referred to his droll son-in-law is not known.

Incidentally, Wagner was, if you asked most people not named Liszt, either thoroughly detestable or merely vile. By nearly all accounts, he was mean, violent, notoriously arrogant, overbearing to the point of bullying, and so virulently anti-semitic that, for example, he would only conduct Mendelssohn's works while wearing gloves, which he would remove and cast away at the end of each concert.

Chopin, whom we associate with the sweet innocence of études and nocturnes, was for nine years the lover of novelist George Sand, a fact that becomes either more or less lurid when you know that "George Sand" was the pen name of female novelist Aurore Dudevant.

Schubert's official cause of death was typhoid fever, but some historians say that he was actually felled by syphilis. Schubert was never a conductor, but even so, he may have been undone by poor usage of the baton.

It may not qualify as scandalous, but both Tchaikovsky and Schumann originally studied to become *lawyers* before committing themselves to music. Their change of heart (and career) is a blessing to posterity in more ways than one, since, as we all know, music hath charms to soothe the savage breast, while lawyers merely *sue* the savage breast.

Classic Hard Luck Stories: Being a great musical talent was no insurance against misfortune, malady, or other serious career setbacks, especially with medicine being what it was back then.

Bach, for instance, went blind in later life. So did **Handel,** in 1753, but he continued to compose with British collaborator John C. Smith serving as his eyes and pen. **Beethoven** began suffering a hearing impairment at 30 that grew progressively worse, but he went right on composing great music even after he had gone stone deaf. And **Schumann** went crazy.

Schubert died at a grievously premature 31 years of age from either typhoid or a sexually transmitted disease, depending on whom you believe. **Chopin** was dead at 38, but at least he lasted longer than **Mozart,** who went at age 35, after a soap opera of a life, with four of his six children going young to *their* graves, and bankruptcy an almost constant threat.

Jean Baptiste **Lully,** France's top musician, conductor, and opera director, kept the beat while conducting by loudly banging a large wooden staff on the floor. During one performance, he mashed his foot on a particularly vigorous downstroke. The injury became infected, the infection spread, and Lully died. This was a highly persuasive argument in favor of adopting the baton.

If a musical composition can be said to have gotten a raw

deal, that definitely applies to Georges **Bizet**'s first symphony, which he wrote at age 17 in 1855 and then, having decided that he didn't like it, tucked it away where nobody would find it. Which nobody did, until 1938, when it was finally played for the first time—to good reviews.

The Current Class of Classical

THEY MAY NOT BE as familiar as Michael Jackson, Celine Dion, or Kenny G, but the world of classical music has its own name-in-lights artists and performers. Not enough to fill a shuttle bus admittedly, and with but a shadow of the name recognition of their peers in the pop, rock, hip-hop, and country genres, but looming as large on their musical landscape as Gloria Estefan or George Michael do on theirs.

Here are some of the current superstars of classical music—with apologies to the fans of all those classical artists so callously and unjustly overlooked. What they have in common are extraordinary talent, singular popular appeal, and unusual names.

Van Cliburn was born Harvey Lavan Cliburn Jr. in 1934, and it's not hard to see why he made the change. America's most eminent classical pianist, he made his debut with the Houston Symphony at age 13 and played Carnegie Hall the following year. In 1958 he became the first American to win the International Tchaikovsky Competition in Moscow and the first to achieve international superstar stature at the classical keyboard. His performance of Tchaikovsky's *Piano Concerto No. 1* became the first long-play classical recording to sell a million copies, in 1961. He's particularly noted for his way with the works of late Romantic period composers. He would probably be the biggest concert draw in classical music today but stopped performing in public in 1978.

Luciano Pavarotti, tenor, was born in Modena, Italy, in 1935, the first and only son of a baker. Sports occupied much of his time as a boy. In fact, he earned his first local fame excelling on his town's soccer team, a sport he has followed fervently ever since. He first sang in the Modena chorus with his father, an avid lover of opera and gifted amateur tenor. When the chorus won first prize in an international competition, the young Pavarotti was hooked. His debut came on April 29, 1961, as Rodolfo in *La Boheme*, at the opera house in Reggio Emilia Romagna. His American debut came in February 1965, in a Miami production of *Lucia di Lammermoor* with Joan Sutherland, the beginning of what would become their historic partnership. On February 17, 1972 the Pavarotti phenomenon was born, in a production of *La Fille du Regiment* at New York's Metropolitan Opera. In response to Pavarotti's aria, featuring nine effortless high C's (don't try this at home), the audience erupted in a frenzied ovation, and Lucky Luciano's reputation achieved liftoff.

Placido Domingo is considered, along with Luciano Pavarotti, one of the world's two greatest opera singers. Born in Madrid in 1941 to two successful performers of Spanish operettas, Domingo has had a professional career spanning more than four decades. He has given more than 27,000 performances and has been featured in over 100 opera recordings. Domingo made his opera debut in 1957 as a baritone in the zarzuela *Gigantes y cabezudos* in Mexico. When he was offered a contract by an opera company in Mexico City if he would change his vocal range to tenor, he agreed. In February 1966 he sang the title role in the American premiere of Alberto Ginastera's *Don Rodrigo* with the New York City Opera, and became a celebrity. In 1990 he took the stage for the first time with Luciano Pavarotti and José Carreras at the World Cup Soccer Championship in Rome. They were billed as "The Three Tenors" and instantly became classical music's first supergroup.

Richard Stolzman, clarinet virtuoso, was born in Omaha, Nebraska, in 1942. His father bought him his first clarinet when he was 7, but he wasn't introduced to classical music until the early 1960s while at Ohio State University majoring in math and music. In 1973 he formed a quartet with violinist Ida Kavafian, cellist Bill Sherry, and pianist and composer Bill Douglas. The quartet called themselves Tashi, Tibetan for "good fortune," which is what they had with *Quartet for the End of Time,* their first recording. The following year, Stolzman made his New York debut as a solo recitalist and his recording debut that same year with an album entitled *A Gift of Music for Clarinet,* an understatement. In 1982 he gave the first solo clarinet performance ever presented in Carnegie Hall.

James Galway strolls onstage shouldering his flute like a rifle. He's also armed with an easygoing manner that charms concertgoers, and an extraordinary range and virtuoso technique that holds them spellbound. Galway was born in 1945 in Belfast, Northern Ireland. He received his first flute at age 8, and took to it with a passion he still exhibits today. An alumnus of the Royal Philharmonic Orchestra at the Berlin Philharmonic, he began a successful solo career in 1975 and continues to delight international audiences.

Leontyne Price is a rags-to-riches story worthy of an opera in its own right. The first (born in 1927) and foremost in a remarkable line of African-American divas (which simply means "distinguished female singer"), she rode her extraordinary vocal range, power, purity, and emotion all the way from Laurel, Mississippi, to the world stage, becoming one of the first eminences of televised opera in the 1950s (despite some network affiliates' resistance on racial grounds), as well as the first great classical vocal recording star, winning Grammies like they were carnival prizes—18 in all. She virtually defined the title role in *Aida*, and retired, still atop the game, in 1985.

Jessye Norman, African-American soprano, was born in Augusta, Georgia, in 1945. In 1969 she made her debut in *Tannhauser* with the Berlin Opera, and was a great success as Aida at London's Covent Garden and Milan's La Scala in 1972. In 1982 she made her American debut as Jocasta in *Oedipus Rex* and her Metropolitan Opera debut the following year as Cassandra in *Les Troyens*. Norman, as one of the most acclaimed musical artists of the late 20th century, commands a broad operatic repertoire and frequently performs concerts of spirituals, oratorios, and a variety of other works. She has been praised for her enormous vocal power, tonal warmth, and clarity of diction.

Itzhak Perlman was born in Tel Aviv in 1945. He was four years old when two events shaped his life: He was afflicted with polio, losing the use of his legs, and he took up the violin. For someone who can stand only with braces, he casts one of the longest shadows in classical music. He made his debut at Carnegie Hall at age 17 and the following year won gigs with the New York Philharmonic. Since then he has recorded just about every major classical string composition of the last two centuries, and is easily America's premier classical violinist, if not the world's. His strengths are a tremendous expressiveness, dazzling technique, and mastery of detail. Like cellist Yo Yo Ma, he's a crossover artist who has also recorded everything from Scott Joplin ragtime to Andre Previn jazz compositions, and is so affable and unpretentious that he may even edge Ma on the likability meter.

Andre Watts, a brilliant American pianist, was born in 1946 to a black American soldier and a Hungarian woman. Watts made his first public appearance at age 9 with the Philadelphia Orchestra. At age 16, he played Liszt's *First Piano Concerto,* conducted by Leonard Bernstein with the New York Philharmonic, making him an instant celebrity. His youth and (for classical music) unusual ethnicity may have added to his success, but overall, it was the sheer impact of his virtuosity that won over the usually skeptical press.

Kathleen Battle, African-American soprano, was born in Portsmouth, Ohio, in 1948. She studied voice at the University of Cincinnati's Conservatory of Music and made her debut at the Spoleto Festival in 1972. In 1977 Battle made her New York debut in *The Marriage of Figaro* and a year later debuted in *Tannhauser* at the Metropolitan Opera. Known for her clear, pure voice, she has also acquired a reputation for her temperamental behavior and was dismissed from the Metropolitan in 1994 for her unprofessional behavior.

Yo Yo Ma, a.k.a. the best cellist alive, has an odd name even for a great artist. (Still, it's probably better than Whoopi or Hootie if you plan to play the Kennedy Center.) Born in Paris in 1955 to a musicologist father, he was playing recitals at age five, and has consistently grown and improved ever since. He plays more Bach than almost anyone, and better Bach than everyone, and his classical works are heavily weighted with chamber music and small-ensemble string compositions. But he's also as eclectic and experimental as a Miles Davis; in three years he produced highly successful recordings of bluegrass (*Appalachia Waltz,* 1996), ballroom dance music (*Soul of the Tango,* 1997), and baroque suites (*Inspired by Bach,* 1998). Along with flawless technical brilliance and terrific tonal feeling, he has an engaging charm that has made him an admirable ambassador for classical string music.

Wynton Marsalis, trumpeter, composer, and bandleader, was born in 1961 in New Orleans to a distinguished African-American jazz family. He studied classical music at the Juilliard School in New York. Marsalis, who is articulate, outspoken, and considered one of the leading jazz musicians of the 1980s and '90s, has compiled serious credentials in the world of classical music as well, earning strong reviews for *Tomasi/Jolivet Trumpet Concertos, Wynton Marsalis Plays Baroque Music for Trumpets* (both 1988), and *In Gabriel's Garden* (1996).

Nadja Salerno-Sonnenburg is a gifted American violinist of Russian-Italian descent. Born in Rome in 1961, she went to New York to study at the Juilliard School at the age of 14. After winning the Naumberg Competition in 1981, she dropped out of Juilliard, sans diploma, to launch an independent career. Salerno-Sonnenburg has become a popular figure in the media, due in large part to her non-conformist persona, disdain for conventional attire, and impassioned stage presence. Her violin performances demonstrate a genuine talent to be reckoned with.

Classic Overachievers

Fastest composer: Schubert (the composer, not the frozen non-dairy dessert) produced more than 1,000 works in 18 years and change, and routinely turned out a complete composition in a day.

Fastest musician: Nicolo Paganini had a reputation as the most rapid violinist in history and was officially clocked at more than 12 notes per second, which almost qualifies him as a trio. Today, he would presumably be doing FedEx commercials.

Fastest out of the box: Whatever the specific musical form, the record holder for Earliest Composition is likely to be Mozart, who wrote a minuet at the age of four and had written 30 symphonies by the time he was 20. But Mozart was really just the most extreme example of a virtual infestation of prodigies that marked the classical music era. Liszt was an accomplished pianist at age seven, and began composing at eight; he was playing concerts a year later. Mendelssohn was turning out violin masterpieces when he was 12. Schubert had compiled a virtual career by age 20. It's easy and tempting to come to the conclusion that the 18th and 19th centuries were some kind of Age of Child Geniuses. But remember, these were basically kids with limited creative options and lots of free time. Take away TV, video games, movies, sports, computers, rock and roll, rap music, and the like, and you'd probably have 10-year-olds knocking out concertos today. At least you wouldn't have Britney Spears. And even with all that we still get prodigies, like violinist Sarah Chang, who did a guest appearance with the New York Philharmonic at age 8 to a standing ovation.

Biggest hands: The average hand, from pinkie to thumb-tip, can stretch about one octave—eight white keys—on the piano. Most piano professionals can cover 10. But the largest official recorded hand-span is credited to the great classical pianist, Sergei Rachmaninoff—12 keys. Granted, there may be somebody in the NBA who could top that if he tried; but who knows, if Rachmaninoff were alive today, he might be a terrific ball handler.

Biggest (and for that matter, loudest) ensemble: Gustav Mahler's *Symphony of a Thousand* was designed and written to be performed by, literally, 1,000, and in fact actually has been. The resulting sound is probably formidable, and maybe even magnificent, but between the audience and the performers, the traffic going home must be a nightmare.

Most prolific: Along with the hundreds of symphonies, fugues, cantatas, masses, and sonatas that he churned out, Johann Sebastian Bach fathered 20 kids. Perhaps he was attempting to breed his own orchestra.

Biggest draw: On July 5, 1986, Zubin Mehta conducted the New York Philharmonic in a concert of classical music on the Great Lawn in Central Park, to a crowd estimated at 800,000. This proves that however times and tastes may change, the ordinary person is still strongly attracted to such concepts as "virtuosity" and "grandeur" and "free admission."

Most shelf space: In 2000, the Haenssler Classic company of Stuttgart, Germany, commemorated the 250th anniversary of Bach's death by releasing his collected works, 1,100 compositions in a special collection of 160 compact discs. Total price: $1,380.

Classic Expressions

NOT ONLY HAVE you often heard classical music without knowing it, you've occasionally *talked* classical music without knowing it, thanks to a few phrases that were born in the classical world and migrated out to become part of the popular lexicon. For example:

Downbeat refers to the *beat* that the orchestra conductor sets with the *down* stroke of his baton. Later, the phrase came to mean an unhappy appearance or expression, maybe because that's how a musician who *missed* the downbeat looked after the conductor laid the baton upside his head. Now it is more widely associated with jazz, because let's face it, "downbeat" just *sounds* like a jazz thing.

Second fiddle, referring to the violinist who plays a supporting role to the lead violinist, has become a term that we apply to the number twos and lesser-knowns of the world: Pepsi, Scottie Pippen, almost any vice president, Robin (the Boy Wonder), and Keith Richards (who effectively plays "second fiddle" to Mick Jagger, even though he plays lead guitar in actual fact). Curiously, and for no clear reason, you never hear Coca-Cola, Michael Jordan, the president, Batman, or other "number ones" described as "playing first fiddle."

Longhair music once upon a time referred to the fact that classical composers, for the most part, were not major patrons of the barber shop. People in general were not haircut enthusiasts during the 17th and 18th centuries. This changed in the late 19th and early 20th, however, and it became fashionable among hip, short-haired "moderns" to look upon classical music as old-fashioned stuff left over from when people wore long hair. This mildly derogatory term remained in usage until the 1960s, when the Beatles and Stones and Dylan and everybody who even *owned* a guitar suddenly had hair that made Liszt look like Tony Bennett, thereby confusing the issue thoroughly so that "longhair music" no longer had any coherent meaning.

Horning in comes from early orchestra compositions in which the strings began the music, and then the horns came in, often at such a louder volume as to drown the strings out and take over the piece. This left the string players resentfully fantasizing about sticking the horns where they would be impossible to play (but would be safe from exposure to the sun), and it left us with a phrase that means to thrust oneself into a group or situation or conversation. Of course, if "horning" in originates from using a horn to gain entry into something, the mind can only wonder over the origin of "butting" in.

Classical Ways to Make a Living

ALTHOUGH YOU WON'T see it in *Newsweek's* "Go-Go Careers for the New Millennium" article, classical concert musician is not only a legitimate profession, but also one at which you can do pretty nicely for yourself financially. A musician employed full-time by a major big-city orchestra can earn anywhere from $25,000 to nearly $100,000 per year, depending on the instrument and its prominence (lead violin versus triangle, for instance), the orchestra's status, and the length of its official season, which can range from 29 to 52 weeks per year. Members of the San Francisco Symphony are paid a base scale of $1,550 per week. A majority earn more, and individuals can contract privately for more than scale. The money tends to plummet below that level, but even a regional metro orchestra gig is good for $4,000 to $15,000 annually.

However, unless you're one of the handful of contemporary superstars in classical music—Van Cliburn, Itzhak Perlman, and the like—there is not much money in making classical recordings. Given a scale on which a gold record reflects one million sales, even your most successful classical albums are lucky to rate tin, lead, or even mahogany: 50,000 copies is a major hit, and 75,000 is pretty much the ceiling. And the trend is not upward: In 1992, classical recordings made up 3.7 percent of all music sales; by 1997 their share had sagged to 2.7 percent, the kind of number generally associated with the Learning Channel and the Prohibition Party.

That, of course, is for pure classical music, written by classical composers, and played in the classical manner by traditional classical musicians.

By contrast, when a Paul McCartney releases a "symphony"—as he did with *Liverpool Oratorio* and *Standing Stone*—the result is a crossover hit that kills on both the classical and pop charts, and sells standing-room tickets at Carnegie Hall.

The key to success as a classical musician these days seems to be to conceal as much as possible that you are a classical musician. The best evidence of this is provided by Vanessa-Mae, a fetching classical violin prodigy who pranced into the spotlight at age 15 with a video in which she played a techno-pop take of Bach's *Toccata and Fugue in D Minor* while attired in your traditional wet T-shirt. Her first all-classical album (ingeniously titled *Classical Album 1*), which was released two years later, didn't just go through the roof, but took the roof with it, selling 500,000 copies worldwide in two weeks to take honors as the fastest-selling solo classical album in history.

Accordingly, the future of recordings for classical fans will probably consist mostly of crossover blends of pop musicians playing classical works, or vice versa, in a fusion of pop and classical that purists and nags like to call *popsical,* at least until the Popsicle Company's lawyers contact them. It may not be the finest thing to ever happen to the listener's ears, but it outsells traditional classical nowadays by three to one and growing.

Serious Wannabes

I F YOU FEEL a bit self-conscious about trying to pass yourself off as a knowledgeable lover of classical music, be at
ease. Your pretensions are nothing, compared to those of
some notable personages who are or were *major* classical
music wannabes, to the extent that they have taken serious
flings at performing and/or composing their own legitimate
symphonies and other classical works.

Among performers, you can count **Michael Bolton,** who
released a CD of operatic arias in early 1998 that actually
topped Billboard's classical charts for six weeks and who
may have brought classical opera to a historic low point of
sorts when he warbled the strains of Puccini's *Nessun Dorma*
on the sitcom, *The Nanny.* By contrast, **Aretha Franklin** had
the somewhat better taste to sing the same number at the
Grammys.

Elvis Costello released a CD of classical material performed with the Brodsky Quartet, and **Bobby McFerrin** is
so multi-talented that it shouldn't surprise anyone that he
has conducted the Cleveland Orchestra.

Danny Kaye was wild and wacky, but he also conducted
major symphony orchestras in classical concerts, although
hardly in the classical manner. He was given to lying on his
back and conducting with his feet, using a flyswatter as a
baton, and other stylistic quirks calculated to get Toscanini

whirling in his grave. He claimed he couldn't read a musical note, but critics said his work (or play) lived up to symphonic standards, and Zubin Mehta gave him kudos for "a very efficient conducting style." The idea of Danny Kaye conducting the New York Philharmonic on PBS and winning a Peabody for it might be a stretch, but it happened. Maybe that's what you should expect from the man who starred in *The Secret Life of Walter Mitty.*

Similarly, to you **Shari Lewis** (1934–1998) was probably just that sweet thing on PBS with a sock puppet on one hand, "Lambchop." But in fact she was also a highly accomplished musician and student of music theory and orchestration who, in her spare time, conducted big-league orchestras around the world, including the Pittsburgh Symphony and the National Symphony in Washington, D.C.

Given how convincingly **David Ogden Stiers** played the role of the stuffy and elitist surgeon Major Charles Winchester on *M*A*S*H,* it seems appropriate that he also fancies himself a classical conductor. Word is he's not bad, but he's no Danny Kaye. And the late **Dudley Moore,** the star of *Foul Play, Arthur,* and other films, not only got to roll around on a bed with Bo Derek in *10,* he also turned out to be an accomplished and respected classical concert pianist. Life is not fair.

In the category of wannabe classical composers, we have:

Paul McCartney—You'd think he'd be happy just being a former Beatle and having written the most-recorded and biggest-selling single tune of all time in *Yesterday.* But oh no. He had to go and knock off a pair of symphonies: *Liverpool Oratorio* in 1991, whose resounding obscurity makes it a great trivia question, and his much better-known 1997 composition, *Standing Stone*. Ironically—and perhaps unfortunately—*Stone* is as conservative as some of McCartney's early work with John Lennon was innovative. But it's a pleasant listen and was greeted politely, if not effusively, by the critics. Still, if he'd written it in 1968 or so, the title would probably have been *Lying Stoned*.

Stuart Copland—Formerly the drummer for The Police, he composed an opera for the Cleveland Opera, which may indicate that the city's opera house is too close to the city's Rock and Roll Museum.

Billy Joel—Was said to be composing *only* classical stuff in the late '90s.

These people, of course, are professional musicians, and their attempt at classical composition is reasonable, if a tad uncharacteristic. But you'd be surprised (we hope) at some of the historic personages who've tried their hand at this.

Norodom Sihanouk. The on-and-off king of Cambodia, in between coups, exiles, and revolutions, fancied himself a musical artiste and wrote a number of orchestral compositions, mostly military marches, which made sense given that his country was usually at war with itself or Vietnam. Perhaps he thought of composing as a kind of fallback career (he also played sax in his own jazz band, just in case).

Frederick the Great. Primarily known as the ruler who made Prussia the foremost European power in the 1700s and a genuine military genius (who could forget his epic Seven Years War?), Frederick was also, in his youth, so devoted to music and poetry that his father nearly disowned him as an effeminate fop. In fact, when not busy annexing Silesia or intimidating Austria, he batted out four concertos and 120 sonatas for the flute. Many composers are called "great," but only Frederick holds the actual title.

Richard Coeur de Lion. Not only did Richard the Lion-Hearted lead the armies of Christendom in the Crusades and return to England to oust the evil King John and appear at the end of Robin Hood movies, but he wrote numerous ballads, the key phrase here being "he wrote." The first King Richard was also one of the first composers to actually *write down* his compositions in a form that survives today. Alas, the Lion-Hearted may also have had a bit of the weasel to him, since it is reckoned that many of his "works" were actually popular folks tunes of the period that he, er, "appropriated."

Henry VIII. He's been played by everybody from Charles Laughton to Richard Burton in films that portray him as a spoiled, petulant, gluttonous ass, all of which may be, but just for the record, he composed music that was very well regarded by the peers and nobles of the court, who knew what was good for them. Among his compositions was the old familiar tune "Amaryllis." Alas, though Henry went through wives like they were hats, it appears that he never composed a wedding march.

Schwann Catalog

THIS HAS NOTHING TO DO with bicycles. In fact, the Schwann Opus Catalog is a directory of currently available recorded classical music. To quote its own self-description, "Schwann Opus is the most comprehensive listing of classical recordings available in the U.S. Recognized as the 'definitive reference guide to classical music,' this quarterly publication contains over 45,000 CDs, cassette tapes, and laser discs. Items are organized under composer name, and each piece on the recording is fully listed. Opus also includes timely feature stories and in-depth interviews on influential artists and composers, as well as reviews of hot new releases."

The "hot new releases" part may be a bit hyperbolic, or at least optimistic, but the rest is dead on.

Background: Because it is economically impractical for most stores that sell recorded music to keep a comprehensive classical music inventory on hand, they may instead keep the Schwann on hand, which the classical music consumer can refer to, and then order from through the store. If you want anything but the most general, pop-oriented classical recordings, it is as indispensable as knowing how to say "Extra well done" in a restaurant in Turkey.

It was begun by musicologist, publisher, and record store owner William Schwann in Burlington, Massachusetts, in 1949. The first long-playing records had hit the market in

1948, and were already being produced in such profusion that it was impossible to stay abreast of current (and past) releases. Schwann made up a list of all the available recordings, which ran 26 pages. It soon became an essential item for musicians, record collectors, critics, and recording companies, and Schwann continued to update it. By 1953, this task had grown to the point that he was forced to sell his store and take on a staff devoted just to the now-entrenched Schwann Catalog. Schwann sold the Catalog, which had ballooned to 40,000 entries covering 300 pages, in 1976, but continued to edit and supervise it for some years. Today, the Schwann Opus Catalog is owned by Valley Media in New Mexico, where it is published quarterly and routinely runs 1,000 pages. William Schwann passed away in June 1998 at age 85, his name having become to classical music what Roget and Webster are to literature, but alas, without a similar degree of recognition. Hopefully, someone somewhere will name a small body of water in his honor. Schwann Lake. He'd like that.

Classical Humor

THERE IS NOT a lot of conspicuous jocularity in classical music, but you can find some chuckles if you look
closely enough. A few composers actually had a fairly well-
developed sense of humor. Haydn, for example, once worked
for a particularly tyrannical prince who refused to permit
the musicians in his court orchestra to go home to visit their
wives. So Haydn composed a Farewell Symphony, which
directed the various musicians to march from the concert
hall and leave, one by one, when their parts were finished.
The prince took the hint and relented.

And nothing lays them on the floor at the conservatory
like the one about the time Brahms was playing some hot
piano in a duet with a cellist and the cellist at one point said,
"Softer, I can't hear my cello," and without batting a chord,
Brahms replied, "You're lucky, I can."

Beyond that, are there any classical music jokes? Yes. Will
they make you the life of the party? Probably not, unless the
party is being held in a Victorian drawing room in 1860 or
so. Most jokes about classical music are roughly as *old* as
classical music, and while age may increase one's appreciation of the music, it largely has just the opposite effect with
the jokes. For example . . .

Dialogue between two classical musicians:
"Who was that piccolo I saw you with last night?"
"That was no piccolo, that was my fife."

And:

Why did the symphony harpist marry the accordion player?
Upward mobility.

A man is on safari in a strange land and on the third day out, he hears the sound of drumming. Wherever they go, the sound of the drums follows them, beating constantly. This continues for two days, as his guides become more and more apprehensive and nervous. Finally, the drums suddenly stop. The guides instantly begin to moan and wail with grief and horror. The man grabs one and demands to know, "What's wrong?"
"When the drumming stops," he shudders, "the French horn solo begins."

Sign on a classical music teacher's door:
"Gone to Lunch.
  Bach at 2.
  Offenbach Earlier."

Classical music humor, as you can see, tends to involve wordplay. Classical humor especially loves a good pun. Unfortunately, it is equally enamored of a bad one. Such as:

What do you play on a bass violin?
Salmon Chanted Evening.

And:

What string instrumental piece is always played under-water?
Cello Submarine.

But to give it its due, some classical music humor can be every bit as tasteless and/or gruesome as your contemporary stand-up comic. Like this:

Beethoven has just recently died. Two of his most devoted fans hear an old-wives-tale to the effect that if you sit on a person's grave at midnight under a full moon, you can hear what the deceased is up to in the spirit world. One of them suggests that they put this to a test, but the other is spooked by the whole idea. So the first fellow goes alone to Beethoven's resting place at midnight during the next full moon. The following day, he reports to his fellow disciple: "It was true, Heinrich, I swear! I sat on the master's grave and I could hear him at work!"

"Mein Gott," says his friend. "What was Beethoven doing?"

"Decomposing!"

What do you get when you drop a piano on an army base?
A-flat major.

And finally . . .

How do you fix a broken tuba?
With a tuba glue.

Music Hath Charms

O KAY, BUT TO do precisely what?
    The classic line, which most people misquote, came
from William Congreve in 1697: "Music has charms to soothe
a savage breast / To soften rocks, or bend a knotted oak."
But that last part makes music sound rather like blasting
powder and seems a bit exaggerated.

Of course, Congreve wasn't the only one given to inflat-
ing the benefits of music. The idea of classical music having
therapeutic or healing qualities has been kicking around for
some time. In one notable if unofficial study, Cassandra
Franklin, a leading member of the Grey Ladies (nursing vol-
unteers with the Red Cross), played music to wounded troops
at the Fort Dix Tilton Army Hospital in 1942 in order to
hasten the healing process, and it was reported that the GIs
were up and around remarkably quickly. Of course, this
could simply mean that they were all Glenn Miller fans and
couldn't stand to listen to any more chamber music.

"Music is the Medicine of the Mind."—John Logan
    More recently, there's a theory gaining popularity that
classical music is great fertilizer for the intellect, and the
younger the intellect, the better. This is called the "Mozart
Effect." In 1998, Florida state Senator Bill Turner introduced
legislation to require all state-funded child care centers to

play classical music for their young charges. The senator's belief is that the sound of sonatas enhances the formation of infant brain cell connections, thus producing smarter kids.

And before you say something snotty like, "This guy's parents must have played him a lot of Spike Jones when he was a kid," Senator Turner is not alone.

In the same year, Georgia Governor Zell Miller, who also believes that classical music boosts infant brain development, struck a deal with Sony Music to provide classical CDs and cassettes to the state's 100,000 or so annual newborns.

For more musical quotes to make your dinner conversations snappy, see Nat Shapiro's *An Encyclopedia of Quotations About Music* or Ian Croft's *A Dictionary of Musical Quotations*.

Glossary

A LOT OF THE TERMINOLOGY in classical music can be misleading. For example, *largo* does not refer to one of the Florida Keys, nor is it Spanish for "big." In fact, it's an instruction on sheet music indicating the speed at which the music should be played: *very slow*. Since you're never more than one good verbal screw-up from making a fool of yourself in discussions of classical music, it pays to know, if not precisely what you're talking about, at least what the words that you're using mean.

Feel free to clip this list and pin it inside your top hat.

Absolute music: Music that stands by itself, as opposed to "program music" or "symphonic (tone) poems," which tell a story or describe something beyond the music.

Adagio: A slow, leisurely tempo.

Allegro: A lively, medium-fast tempo.

Alto: The lowest female voices in choral singing.

Aria: A song written for solo voice, usually in an opera or oratorio.

Baroque music: Music written during the latter part of the 17th century or the first half of the 18th.

Bass: The lowest male singing voices in opera, or the deepest of a kind of instrument (bass violin, bass drum).

Cantata: Originally a 17th-century term meaning a musical work written for a single voice accompanied by a cello or harpsichord, relating a story or drama, usually religious. In the 18th century, it expanded to include two or more voices, and a string orchestra.

Chamber music: Compositions designed to be performed in smaller venues than concert halls, especially a room in the home. Mainly associated with string quartets, but ranging from groups of three to eight or nine.

Coda: A climactic musical flourish at the end of a symphony or other composition to close it out emphatically, provide a big finish, and wake everybody up.

Concerto: A composition written for a solo instrument (usually piano or violin) accompanied by an orchestra, and consisting of three movements. Became popular during the Baroque period. One variation is the concerto grosso, for a small *group* of soloists backed by the orchestra.

Contralto: The lowest female voices in opera.

Counterpoint: Playing or singing two or more melodies simultaneously for harmony or to contrast two approaches to the same theme.

Crescendo: Increasing in volume from soft to loud.

Development: 1) Using different harmonies, melodies, or rhythms to elaborate on a basic theme; or, 2) The middle section of a movement that follows the sonata form, where the movement's basic themes are creatively embellished and tinkered with.

Étude: A composition that presents some specific technical challenge, often designed to be played for practice or study.

Exposition: The first section of a sonata form movement, it establishes the primary theme of that movement with a simple tune or melody, then the secondary theme with a slightly more complicated tune or melody, usually repeated.

Forte: Loud. (Note: "Hold the forte" does not mean Soft.)

Fortissimo: Very loud.

Fugue: (Pronounced "Fewg," and we're not going there.) A form of Baroque music in which several instruments play the same basic theme in an overlapping manner, the first one introducing the tune, then the second coming in and repeating the tune while the first voice continues, and so on. The basic example is "Row Row Row Your Boat."

Kapellmeister: Originally the church or court chapel master or musical director; later on, the term for orchestra or choir conductor.

Lied: German for song (or lawyerese for "talked").

Melody: A tune, a song, a series of single notes having a definite rhythm and flow.

Movement: One "chapter" of music within a larger "book" such as a sonata or symphony. A movement usually takes the sonata form and consists of an exposition, a development, and a recapitulation, each of which presents the basic themes of that movement in different ways.

Nocturne: A dreamy, romantic piece, usually written for and performed on the piano.

Opera: A play set to music and sung, performed in costumes and with scenery, to the accompaniment of an orchestra. Not to be confused with any daytime TV talk show hostess seen by far more people.

Operetta: A lighter, more whimsical version of opera, usually with some spoken dialogue; light opera, or, if you like, opera light.

Opus: Latin for "work," used by composers to indicate the order in which they published their compositions: Opus #16, Opus #17, etc.

Glossary

Oratorio: A Baroque period religious composition written for orchestra, chorus, and solo vocalists; think of a choir, singing a story, with an orchestra backing them.

Overture: Originally a piece of music written by the composer to be played immediately before the beginning of an opera to alert the audience that things were about to begin; it later developed into a legitimate, independent musical form composed in its own right.

Pizzicato: There's a truly terrible pun here somewhere involving a feline house pet and an Italian take-out item, but we'd like to maintain at least some dignity, so: Playing a stringed instrument by plucking the strings instead of bowing them.

Presto: More than just the prefix to change-o, it means a fast tempo.

Requiem: Music for a Catholic mass for the dead, usually written for voices and orchestra.

Sonata: A composition, usually written for a solo keyboard or another instrument and keyboard, and consisting of three movements or more. It may follow, but is not limited to, the:

Sonata form: The three-part structure (exposition, development, recapitulation) that makes up one movement in a sonata or a larger instrumental composition, and the basis of most classical works since the Renaissance and Baroque period. Not to be confused with songs about brief flings with dames you loved that just didn't work out, *i.e.* the Frank Sonata form.

Suite: A collection of short instrumental dance tunes grouped together in a kind of set, it was all the rage in the Renaissance and Baroque periods but was out of style by the late 1700s. Its reign was, dare we say, short but suite.

Symphony: Technically, a large-scale composition for a full orchestra, consisting of three or more movements, one or more of which are based on the sonata form. Artistically, the ultimate expression of a composer's abilities in terms of content, sophistication, and artistic goals. Pragmatically, the biggest serving of classical music that you get in one sitting.

Tempo: The speed at which a piece of music is played.

Theme: A series of notes—sometimes the melody—which becomes the basis for development.

Toccata: A virtuoso composition for some keyboard instrument, written to sound improvised.

Tone poem (or symphonic poem): A large-scale orchestral piece that tells a story or reproduces a poem or play musically.

Virtuoso: A musician who is so brilliant and skilled at playing an instrument that even other musicians pay to hear him or her play.

Index

Index

étude, 37
exposition, 8

Fair Maid of the Mill *(Die Schone Mullerin)* (Schubert), 35
Fanfare for the King's Supper (Mouret), 20
Faust (Gounod), 22
Faust Symphony (Liszt), 40
Fifth Symphony (Beethoven), 7, 10, 15, 19, 81
First Piano Concerto (Tchaikovsky), 45, 96
The Flying Dutchman *(Der Fliegende Holländer)* (Wagner), 41
Franklin, Aretha, 105
Franklin, Cassandra, 114
Frederick the Great, 26, 107
From the New World (New World Symphony) (Dvorak), 17
Funeral March (Chopin), 38
Funeral March of a Marionette (Gounod), 22
Für Elyse (Beethoven), 17

Galway, James, 94
Gershwin, George, 13
Gewandhaus Orchestra, 50
Gounod, Charles, 22
Götterdämmerung (Wagner), 41
Grande Valse Brilliante (Waltz No. 1) (Chopin), 18
"Great" *Ninth Symphony* (Schubert), 17, 35
Grieg, Edvard, 12, 18, 21

Habneck, Francois-Antoine, 61
Haenssler Classic company, 100
Handel, George Friedrich: background, 26–27; compositions, 16, 18; health, 90; music on television, 20; religious music, 23
"Hark the Herald Angels Sing" (Mendelssohn), 23
Haydn, Franz Joseph: background, 27–28; compositions, 10, 23; influence on orchestra size, 51–52; religious, 23
Hebrides Overture (Mendelssohn), 16, 37
Henry VIII, 108
homosexuality, 44, 88
Humoresque (Dvorak), 16
Hungarian Rhapsodies (Liszt), 12, 39

Immortal Beloved, 32
Impressionist period, 12
Invitation to the Dance (von Weber), 60
"Italian" *Symphony No. 4* (Mendelssohn), 16

Jesu, Joy of Man's Desiring
(Bach), 17, 23
Joel, Billy, 107
"Joy to the World" (Handel),
23
Jupiter Symphony (Mozart),
31

Kapellmeister, 25, 30, 59, 118
Kaye, Danny, 106

La Boheme (Puccini), 46, 93
La Gioconda (Ponchielli), 21
La Traviata (Verdi), 46
La Vie Parisienne (Offenbach),
43
ländler, 47
Lanner, Joseph, 47, 87
Les Preludes (Liszt), 16, 19
Lewis, Shari, 106
lieder, 35
*Lieutenant Kije Suite, Opus
60* (Prokofiev), 21
Light Cavalry (von Suppé), 22
Liszt, Franz:
background, 39–40;
compositions, 16, 19;
movie about, 88; music in
movies, 19; romantic life,
88; scandals, 42
Lisztomania, 88
Liverpool Oratorio
(McCartney), 104, 106
Lohengrin (Wagner), 21, 22,
41

*London Symphonies (Nos.
93–104)* (Haydn), 28
Lullaby (Brahms), 15, 21
Lully, Jean Baptiste, 57, 90

Ma, Yo Yo, 95, 96
Madame Butterfly (Puccini), 46
The Magic Flute (Mozart), 31
Mahler, Gustav, 35, 55, 63,
86, 99
The Marriage of Figaro
(Mozart), 10, 30, 31, 96
Martini, Johann, 21
Marsalis, Wynton, 82, 97
McCartney, Paul, 104, 106,
107
McFerrin, Bobby, 105
Mehta, Zubin, 55, 66, 84,
100, 106
Mendelssohn, Felix:
background, 36–37;
compositions, 16, 18; as
conductor, 62; religious
music, 23
Messiah (Handel), 16, 23, 27
"A Mighty Fortress Is Our
God" (Bach), 22
The Military March
(Schubert), 18
Military Polonaise (Chopin),
18
Mlada (Rimsky-Korsakov), 18
Modern period, 13
Moonlight Sonata
(Beethoven), 10

Index

Moore, Dudley, 22, 106
Morning (Grieg), 21
Mouret, Jean-Joseph, 20
movement, 8, 118
Mozart and Salieri (Rimsky-
    Korsakov), 87
Mozart, Wolfgang Amadeus:
    background, 28–31;
    compositions, 10, 23;
    death, 86–87; movie about,
    54–55; opera about,
    86–87, religious music, 23;
    Salieri, 86–87
musical instruments 68–76:
    auxiliary, 76; brass, 70–72;
    keyboards, 75–76;
    percussive, 74–75; string,
    72–74; woodwind, 68–70

Nessun Dorma (Puccini), 105
New World Symphony (From
    the New World) (Dvorak),
    17
Ninth Symphony (Beethoven),
    15, 17, 20, 34, 35
Norman, Jessye, 95
The Nutcracker
    (Tchaikovsky), 17, 44

"O God Our Father, Throned
    on High" (Bach), 23
Ode to Joy (Beethoven), 15, 34
Offenbach, Jacques, 10, 43
operas:
    Bizet, 15; Mozart, 86–87;

Offenbach, 43; Ponchielli,
    21; Puccini, 46; Rossini, 45;
    Verdi, 46; Wagner, 41
Opus 51, Number 1
    (Schubert), 18
oratorio, 6, 7, 27, 28, 37, 95,
    104
orchestra(s) 50–56:
    American, 54–55; average
    size, 52; first, 50–51;
    modern, 51; musical instru-
    ments required, 53;
    physical layout, 53
Orchestra Opus No. 64
    (Mendelssohn), 18
orchestration, 52, 61
Ozawa, Seiji, 55, 66

Pachelbel, Johann, 6, 20
Paganini, Nicolo, 98
Passacaglia (Bach), 25
*The Passion According to St.
    Matthew* (Bach), 7
Peer Gynt suites (Grieg), 21
Perlman, Itzhak, 95, 103
Piano Concerto No. 1
    (Tchaikovsky), 45, 92, 96
Piano Concerto No. 2
    (Rachmaninoff), 16
Piano Concerto Opus 16
    (Grieg), 18
Piano Concertos (Grieg), 18
Plaisier d'Amour (Martini), 21
Polonaise No. 6 (Chopin), 12,
    18

polyphony, 5
Ponchielli, Amilcare, 21
Price, Leontyne, 94–95
Procession of the Nobles (Rimsy-Korsakov), 18
Prokofiev, Sergei, 21
Puccini, Giacomo, 45, 46, 105

Rachmaninoff, Sergei, 16, 99
Ravel, Maurice, 2, 12, 22
recapitulation, 8
Reformation Symphony (Mendelssohn), 37
Reichardt, Johann Friedrich, 59
religious music, 22–23
Renaissance period, 5
Requiem (Mozart), 31
restatement, 8
Rhapsody in Blue (Gershwin), 13
Rhenish Symphony (Schumann), 39
Richard the Lion-Hearted, 108
Rigoletto (Verdi), 46
Rimsky-Korsakov, Nikolai, 14, 18, 87
The Ring Cycle *(Der Ring des Nibelungen)* (Wagner), 41
Romantic period, 10–12
Romeo and Juliet (Tchaikovsky), 12, 17, 45
Romeo et Juliette (Gounod), 22

Rossini, Gioacchino, 3, 10, 20, 45, 46

St. John Passion (Bach), 25
St. Matthew Passion (Bach), 25
St. Paul oratorio (Mendelssohn), 37
Salerno-Sonnenburg, Nadja, 97
Salieri, Antonio, 31, 86–87
Scenes from Childhood (Schumann), 17
Scheherazade (Rimksy-Korsakov), 18
Schubert, Franz: background, 35–36; compositions, 16, 17, 18; death, 89, 90
Schumann, Robert: background, 37; compositions, 37, 42; death, 37; insanity, 55; scandals, 55
Schwanengesang (Swan Song) (Schubert), 35
Schwann Opus Catalog, 109–110
The Seasons (Haydn), 28
Shaw, Robert, 65–66
Shostakovich, Dmitri, 2
Sihanouk, Norodom, 107
Sleeping Beauty (Tchaikovsky), 17, 44
sonata, 8

Index

Also available from RDR Books